To my dear friend, Doris, who
" plays house" every day.
Fondly, Doris
Christmas 1999

THE VIVIEN GREENE
DOLLS' HOUSE COLLECTION

THE VIVIEN GREENE DOLLS' HOUSE COLLECTION

Vivien Greene

with Margaret Towner

Photographs by Nick Nicholson

THE OVERLOOK PRESS
WOODSTOCK • NEW YORK

First published in 1995 by
Cassell, London
First published in the United States in 1995 by
The Overlook Press
Lewis Hollow Road
Woodstock, New York 12498

Library of Congress Cataloging-in-Publication Data

Greene, Vivien.
  [Dolls' house]
  The Vivien Greene Dolls' House Collection : the complete Rotunda Collection
  Vivien Greene, Margaret Towner.
     p.   cm.
  Includes index.
  ISBN 0-87951-632-1
  1. Dollhouses – England – History – 18th century – Catalogs.
2. Dollhouses – England – History – 19th century – Catalogs. 3. Greene, Vivien – Art collections – Catalogs. 4. Dollhouses – Private collections – England – Oxford – Catalogs. 5. Dollhouses – England – Oxford – Catalogs. 6. Rotunda Museum of Antique Doll's Houses (Oxford, England) – Catalogs. I. Towner, Margaret. II. Rotunda Museum of Antique Doll's Houses (Oxford, England) III. Title.
NK4894.G7G74 1995
688.7'23'094297442574–dc20
                95-18107
                CIP

Printed in Italy

Half title page. This air-twist wine glass, less than 1in (2.5cm) high, was given to me when I was nine years old and was the start of the whole collection.

Frontispiece. The grandiose hall of the Edwardian Villa has a fine staircase dividing on to two galleries. Under the staircase are pillared arches, a popular feature at that date (known as 'Liberty Arches', because they could be purchased at Liberty's shop). The banisters are elaborately turned. On the rear wall is a large pipe organ; it does not have a keyboard but is powered by a musical box! At the front is a German carved wooden bear, a feature still popular at the time and often used to hold a lamp, a bearskin rug, suits of armour and hunting trophies.

CONTENTS

LIST OF DOLLS' HOUSES

Preface

In 1948, following a visit to the Greg Collection of dolls' houses in Manchester, the curator said to me: 'Another girl who's writing a book about dolls' houses was here a few weeks ago.' The 'other girl' was, of course, Vivien Greene. Except for a learned turn-of-the-century volume about the Dutch Puppenhuisen and *The Book of the Queen's Dolls House* in 1924, there had never been a book about dolls' houses. In one of those coincidences which are always so intriguing, two books were on their way.

A number of years passed before this writer crossed the ocean again and met her fellow dolls' house historian – who became a treasured friend. Visits have been exchanged – and many letters. Inasmuch as the author of this exquisite book cannot write an uninteresting word, her letters are treasured, along with the miniature architecture and artefacts we have mutually pursued for half a century.

It is with delight that we, her readers, welcome this volume, which is graced not only by her luminous words – enhanced by the dedicated and caring research of Margaret Towner – but also by Nick Nicholson's elegant illustrations. The latter provide the only dimension that had eluded this splendid collection until now: full colour, at long last.

FLORA GILL JACOBS
Director, Washington Dolls' House & Toy Museum, Washington, DC

Introduction

by Margaret Towner

The title 'collector' has always had a little barb attached to it. When, in the seventeenth century, it became fashionable to amass curiosities, the collector had something of the reputation of a magician or an alchemist, hoarding objects peculiar rather than valuable or beautiful, with stuffed crocodiles suspended from the ceiling. Nevertheless, Elias Ashmole's private museum became the Ashmolean in Oxford, and Sir Hans Sloane's assemblage of 'Plants, Corralls, Minerals, Earth, Shells, Animals' eventually became the foundation of the British Museum and the Natural History Museum in London. Royalty and very rich people have always surrounded themselves with expensive and exquisite things, to enhance their position and provide an enjoyable background for their lives, but have frequently been accused of thoughtless extravagance, or of acquiring fashionable items without knowledge of, or affection for, them. Nevertheless, the disposal of these grand collections, such as that of Charles I during the Commonwealth, or Sir Robert Walpole's to Catherine the Great, have caused much lamentation, which in these two cases lingers even now.

The passionate collector has, however, made a contribution to the understanding of art and history which is not always fully appreciated. The world of scholars, museums and dealers is too often bounded by the understood areas of pleasant exploration, as was the classical world by the limits of civilization, beyond which were only barbarians and the boundless ocean. The collector more often begins by seeing and acquiring something strange, usually of little or unknown value, out of curiosity, or because the unusual has a charm of its own. From examining the object, and trying to find out more about its origins,

the interest deepens, and more of a similar kind are sought in shops, markets, auctions and even the dustbins of the neighbours. The collector soon discovers, first, that there are no useful books on the subject of his or her interest, and then that it is difficult to obtain items because, as the shopkeeper traditionally says, 'There is no demand.' People remark, when the subject is mentioned, 'Oh, we found some of those in the old house when Aunt Jane died, but they were very dirty so we put them on the bonfire.' Sometimes this sort of response makes the collector ashamed of the interest, so the collection becomes a secret hoard, hidden even from friends and family. Sooner or later, however, like-minded people emerge and a correspondence begins, meetings are held and perhaps the collector publishes an article in a magazine. Once a small exhibition has taken place, dealers, auctioneers and eventually museum curators and popular writers on art or antiques discover a new and rewarding field.

Many neglected, unknown or unfashionable subjects have been brought back to life in this manner, from Victorian furniture to treen. Vivien Greene has been almost single-handedly responsible for awakening an interest, both aesthetic and historical, in the antique English dolls' house. She is precisely the kind of passionate, curious collector described above.

While Vivien Greene herself describes in some detail how this awakening occurred (see pages 11–15), an understanding of what a particularly deserted area she explored can provide a background against which to view her achievement. The development of an historical approach to English and Continental dolls' houses provides the context to Vivien Greene's work, and some account of this is given here. Also, because her first book, *English Dolls' Houses*, has been out of print for some years, we have decided to include a short extract from it (see pages 184–8), describing the development of the English dolls' house and its contents from 1700 to 1900, as a background to the detail of the houses in the collection. This extract has been updated only in so far as is necessary to cover some further thoughts on a few details which Vivien and others have had during the last forty years. At the end of the book will also be found a glossary of some of the architectural and other technical terms used in the description of the houses in the collection. The collection itself, of course, forms the major part of the book, being a detailed tour in photographs and words of the houses, which together cover a period of 200 years, from about 1700 to 1900.

Vivien Greene has consciously limited her interest to this period and to English houses, because she found them neglected, and because their beauty and individuality were greatest at this time, after which commercial production became entirely dominant. In her writings she has always conveyed very clearly the message that the early houses need to be seen not only as beautiful antique objects but also as microcosms of social history, preserving, sometimes untouched, aspects of domestic life that have been totally overlaid in real old houses by the changes inevitably introduced by centuries of human occupation. She has thus very consistently made the case for antique houses to be treated with respect, and not changed in ways that would destroy their authenticity.

Sadly, it is not possible to say that her ideas have been universally accepted. The introduction of the dolls' house into the collecting field has unfortunately been the cause of the destruction of many fine houses. This has occurred partly through ignorance and partly through greed. While the houses were tucked away in attics or former nurseries, although they were perhaps suffering from damp or woodworm, they were at least intact. Many have since been damaged. This is a problem affecting dolls' houses in particular, rather than antiques generally, or even other types of antique toy. People who inherit eighteenth-century English furniture do not commonly remove the patina and repaint with enamel; the collectors of old tinplate toys regard most highly their original finish, and consider repainting as a last resort, knowing that it greatly reduces the toy's value. Old dolls, in the early days of collecting, did suffer from the ignorant removal of their original clothes and wigs, but most owners now, informed by excellent books, are careful to preserve their dolls intact.

The situation regarding dolls' houses is not so happy. Some have been acquired by families seeking a status toy for their children and 'modernized' with paint and structural alterations. Others have been purchased by adult collectors of modern miniatures who have sacrificed the old paintwork and paper to provide a pristine, smart appearance to match the new furniture. Houses that have survived with their original furniture have had this removed for separate sale by the auction rooms, because this will increase the overall price obtained, even though it destroys a unique piece of history. Museums are far from blameless. Some remove furniture without recording its original position in a room, or lose boxes of furniture, or misguidedly repaint or repaper, taking the view that it 'would be a good idea for the old house to be taken out of store and done up for the children at Christmas'. Many fine houses bequeathed to museums are left indefinitely in store, sometimes in poor conditions.

There have, however, been gains as well as losses, and for these Vivien Greene has been very greatly responsible. Since 1955, when she published her first book, many people have been encouraged to collect, study and conserve old houses which might otherwise have been consigned to the bonfire. Societies have been formed, exhibitions held and further research carried out. Although Vivien Greene's enthusiasm has always been for the eighteenth and nineteenth centuries, when dolls' houses had their greatest individuality, later collectors have taken an interest in the commercially manufactured houses of this century, whether German, British or American. These too have great value as records of aspects of modern social history, and sometimes also have an endearing charm, so many of them may avoid being discarded in an increasingly careless world.

The Love of Houses

by Vivien Greene

HOUSES: the word to me has the same valued and beloved sound as the word 'home'. Home means one's loved place; houses embraces many loved places.

Houses have influenced my life so deeply. They have entered into dreams, have made me stand enraptured, suddenly, in unexpected places, filled me with a longing to possess; or they occasionally frighten. In the strange way in which certain objects – here speaks the collector – gravitate towards anyone who will love them, I have been fortunate in living in houses previously occupied by interesting people. Possibly, as a footnote, the house in Antwerp where I, then aged six, saw for several minutes the apparition of a naked child. Even the house in Beaumont Street, which was, in the late nineteenth century, part of an hotel where Henry James stayed on a visit to Oxford, and now my present house in Iffley, where Mrs Jemima Newman and her daughters lived when her son John Henry Newman, later Cardinal, was Vicar of St Mary's. One room was traditionally his study, and afterward Sir George Forrest wrote his history of the Indian Mutiny there.

Because of his job, my father was constantly moving, and we lived in what seemed an endless number of different towns in England and abroad. We went to Long Ashton, Bristol, Liverpool, Antwerp, Munich; no sooner had we arrived than it seemed to be time to move on again. I was miserable and grew to hate the impermanence of our life and to long above all for a settled home.

From this longing grew, I think, my enduring interest in houses and their contents. Among my happiest times as a child was when, at the age of about eight, I was sent to stay with my maternal grandparents, living in Clifton, an elegant Regency town perched above the Avon Gorge. They, of course, lived a life which was essentially Victorian. My grandfather was a solicitor, and every morning before he went to work we had morning prayers; he read the prayers to the family and the two maids, and then went to the office. His interests were antiquarian: he collected antiques and wrote articles on old Bristol. He took me to see the old buildings in Bristol. The city then retained many ancient houses dating from its early prosperity as a great sea port and trading centre, most of which were eventually bombed during the Second World War.

In my grandparents' home there was a big library and much interesting furniture. I remember a vast piece topped with black marble, reputed to have come originally from the sale of Beckford's Gothick Revival Fonthill Abbey; an old circular table in the drawing room had drawers all round which would have been used in an estate office to receive rents; and a blond wood work-table with all the little bone needlework tools, which fascinated me. I still have the work-table. At teatime a heavy Benares-ware brass tray would be brought up to the drawing room, with toys for me to play with. I remember the solitaire set with its marbles, and the dolls' blue and white dinner service, which I still have. I also had a teddy bear, which was given to me when we were in Liverpool when I was about five, so it was quite an early bear, as bears go. There was also a doll's pram, which in one of those inexplicable but never forgotten tragedies of childhood suddenly disappeared. I was told that it had been given to Cousin Mary.

None of the other houses we lived in when I was a child had such happy memories, but rather later, when I was a teenager and my parents had separated, my mother took a house in Hampstead, and this was the nicest we found. It was 'Capo di Monte', a Regency cottage on Upper Terrace, the last house in a terrace of

'Capo di Monte'

three, and right on the edge of Hampstead Heath. Even Nicklaus Pevsner is unusually rapturous about it, calling it 'that bijou of a cottage'. By tradition it had been lived in by Sarah Siddons, and without any research my mother painted 'S.S.' and a late eighteenth-century date (i.e. when Sarah Siddons had at least lived in Hampstead), and they were still there when I saw the house again in the 1970s! It was rather basic: a bathroom with a glass roof had been tacked on across the tiny paved yard. Much later I was married from there. The house was afterwards bought and occupied by the writer Marghanita Laski. It is also mentioned in the autobiography of Kenneth Clark, the art historian, who found it a romantic retreat in wartime, but soon too small and too damp.

For some time after we married, Graham and I did not have a great deal of money, but in about 1934 we were able to take a house on Clapham Common, and this became a much-loved home. This was No. 14 North Side, part of a terrace built in 1714–20 by a carpenter, John Hutt. Several beautiful early Georgian terraces from this period survive in and around London: for example, Church Row, Hampstead. They were built as retreats for merchants and others from the noise of the city but are entirely urban in character. This house had a carriage entrance, an arch through to the rear, now bricked up, over which are the builder's initials in stone. Inside there was a wonderful staircase, curved and

clinging to the wall, with a big glass dome over it. It had been occupied in the early 1800s by Zachary Macaulay, the father of Lord Macaulay, the historian.

Then came the Second World War and I had to leave London with my two young children. We went, together with the cook and the nanny, to stay with my in-laws in Crowborough. This did not work very well, so after a while I wrote to Stella Weaver, the wife of the President of Trinity College, Oxford, asking if she could find us anywhere to live and she very kindly offered me rooms in the President's lodging. Then one day in October 1940, Graham came with the news that No. 14 North Side had been badly bombed, that it was uninhabitable and we had lost most of our possessions there, including our books. I was devastated and burst into tears. For some time afterwards I tried to find somewhere to live, so that I could move out of Trinity College; then I found a little house in Ship Street, and after that moved to Beaumont Street, a big house which was difficult to run.

14 North Side, Clapham Common

As our furniture and books had been lost, and you could not buy new things in the shops during the war, I took to going to auction sales in the area with A.J.P. Taylor, the historian, to furnish Beaumont Street. One day I went to Burford, saw and was captivated by a dolls' house. I bought it and brought it home on the bus. I needed a hobby, the wartime evenings in the black-out were long and dark, so I started to furnish the house, to make carpets and curtains for it. There was, of course, no question of using new dolls' house miniatures; I never saw such a thing until after the war in America. Roger Warner, the antique dealer, helped me and told other dealers about my interest. I was offered houses for £10 or £12, and antique furniture. At that time no one was interested at all and people offered me free houses. It was common to hear that the old furniture had been given to children in the village. There was one house in a school at Bix, which had a fine staircase, totally destroyed by being used as a cupboard into which the children threw their wellington boots.

Quite soon I started to research, travelling by bus and train, and following up any leads I could find. It was all done via personal contacts, through friends of friends. When I heard of a possible house, I would write to the owner, asking if I could visit to see it. During and after the war it was difficult to get film for a camera, so I filled notebook after notebook with drawings and descriptions of some 1,500 dolls' houses, excluding those of lesser interest, sometimes employing the local photographer to take pictures for me. Often it was very frustrating, if people did not reply to my letters, but sometimes I had happy or amusing experiences. When I visited Norfolk, the places I went were miles from anywhere, empty country with dead pheasants by the roadside. I saw Ann Sharp's seventeenth-century baby house, whose owner, Mrs Bulwer, was then herself 101 and lively as a flea. I also visited a remote farmhouse, where the nice farmer's wife showed me a house, probably eighteenth century, which was entirely different on each side; it looked Dutch, with deep gables.

When I wrote to the owner of Uppark, asking if I could see and measure the grand baby house, Lady Fetherstonhaugh replied, asking me to lunch, to see if I was a suitable person to see it! I stayed with a friend nearby and spent two days at Uppark, seeing how they were repairing the marvellous eighteenth-century curtains, backing the red silk with the finest toile on tables 20 feet long and washing them in Lady Fetherstonhaugh's special saponaria recipe. She had found the little statues that go on top of the baby house somewhere in the stables and was repairing the contents. I was not allowed to take photographs and had to promise not to write about the house; this was a private home. At least after the dreadful fire in 1989 the baby house survived, but there is little that is private now at Uppark.

After the war, when the children were at boarding school, I was able to travel further afield during term-time. I went to Denmark, Sweden, France, America, Austria several times and Germany eight or nine times. I also went to Cape Town, to see the finest collection of baby-house silver toys, Dutch and English.

I had, of course, been collecting dolls'-house furniture as well as houses. A great friend of mine, Valentine Acland, who lived with Sylvia Townsend Warner, took me to a house in Dorset, where there were shelves and shelves of furniture. I was able to buy pieces for about 10 shillings (50p) each, and this formed the principal basis of my collection. I was fascinated by the furniture in Biedermeier style, which I thought at the time resembled the American furniture of Duncan Phyffe; this name stuck to the furniture for some time among collectors, because of its mention in my first book. But for a long time I didn't know the real origin of this manufacturer. Then one day I found in a museum two pieces with gold-stencilled views of castles in trees; a piano that was marked 'Waltershausen' and another piece that was marked 'Reinhardtsbrunn'. They had obviously been made as souvenirs. I looked up these places in a gazetteer and found them in Thüringia, in the then German Democratic Republic. This was in 1962 and at the time the Iron Curtain was at its most impenetrable. It took me almost a year to get a visa; there was no embassy in Britain.

Eventually I reached and negotiated Checkpoint Charlie late one night in March, and I was conveyed after infinite delays to my accredited hotel. For the next six days I walked to and from the Politzei and

THE LOVE OF HOUSES

The Rotunda Museum, opened in 1962.

Interior of the Rotunda Museum.

the Ministry of Culture, to obtain a travel permit. (The nice but stern head of department at the Ministry of Culture came years afterwards to stay a few nights at Grove House with me, totally relaxed and quite merry in the different atmosphere.) Finally I was permitted to buy a train ticket to Gotha: I would be allowed to visit other towns where I might find information about the toy-furniture-makers in whom I was interested, but if I stayed the night I had to report to the local police station. A long and hungry train journey to Gotha followed, where I was assigned a cubicle in a youth hostel. It was awful, so next morning I went to the large and excellent bookshop in the town and sought help. The owner was delightful; I must admit my husband's name was useful. I was invited to tea by an English teacher who wanted to hear what an 'Oxford accent' was (she was fascinated by my description of Nancy Mitford's 'U and Non-U' use of words in the English language) and we had, as a great treat, two tomatoes with our tea. After day trips to various other towns, I was fortunate to obtain an introduction to a retired museum curator of Schloss Tenneberg in Waltershausen. A mysterious tram ride through the pine woods brought me there and – to be brief – in the attics of the Schloss, dusty, unused and piercingly cold, in fading daylight, I was shown dozens of oilcloth-covered albums, the *Musterbuchs* (sample books) for the toy furniture, many beautifully hand-painted, numbered and sometimes priced per dozen dozen. I arranged to have some of the earlier patterns photographed and they were sent to me as microfilm, in exchange for a present of some art books, to avoid the insurmountable currency difficulties.

By this time, of course, I was no longer living in Beaumont Street. When I discovered Grove House, it was owned by Colonel House of Queen's College, who did not wish to sell but offered a lease. However, I did not ever again want to live somewhere on an imper-

manent basis. Six years later, Colonel House became head of Wellington College and Grove House was at last acquired. The house is late eighteenth century, and very pretty, with its veranda and canopy, but it had become very dilapidated during and since the war, needing extensive renovation – floors, ceilings, wiring, heating, etc. It has been my home ever since.

The collection of course grew, and I kept about twelve houses in a bedroom, just standing on the floor. Especially when my first book was published, a lot of people asked to see the dolls' houses. I had the idea for a pavilion in the garden in which to display the houses and was eventually able to engage an architect. He had never designed a museum before, but suggested that if the building were circular, there would be more space for the money, and this was the origin of the Rotunda. A car-hoist was incorporated to lift the houses to the first floor, but the architect had not designed a staircase. I decided that a spiral one would fit in best and advertised for one. A man arrived in a lorry as a result, bringing a section of the staircase used by the actors to reach the stage of the St James's Theatre, recently demolished. This fitted perfectly. The architect would have liked a steel balustrade round the first-floor gallery, but I found a firm in Watlington that still sand-cast iron, and had them use one of the staircase banisters to make a mould. I decorated the inside of the roof with stripes in pink and blue, like a tent.

When the Rotunda was finished, I had a party to open it. Sir Albert Richardson PPRA, performed the opening and I made an iced cake in the shape of the building. The collection has given me immense pleasure ever since, and I have never ceased visiting to see houses elsewhere and making notes. In this way, I have most happily been able to combine having a loved permanent home and indulging, in miniature, my enjoyment of all kinds and periods of English domestic architecture and decoration.

A. Verbeck & Cie

Place Verte, 5.³

Anvers.

Vivien Greene and her brother.

THE COLLECTION

The houses have been arranged in the order of the approximate date of construction. This order can be only tentative since, except in the very rare case of a house with an inscribed date or a documented history, it is based on stylistic evidence alone and, as explained on pages 184–8, a house may be made in the fashion of the time of construction or may be many years in arrears of current architectural taste.

Collecting is not acquiring. It is more like planning a delightful small party, where everyone will find a friend and feel at home. Collecting should be thought of as tenderly as gardening. For that activity, of course, certain physical attributes are needed, but none are needed for collecting . . . not always even the ability to travel, although this naturally adds to the excitement. One remembers the many Syrian dealers bidding for the beautiful rugs and, at the end, the great dolls' house, an eight-foot high castle, which no one wanted and no auction could reasonably accommodate.

Inside was an alabaster chimney piece with the original papers and a built-in pump. In the Gothic windows were ludicrous blinds, complete with tassels. One bid, then mine of £25 secured it. A particular charm lay in the tall, narrow Vauxhall glass mirrors in the drawing room, and strangely, there were already two, precise in proportion, on each side of where the dolls' house finally stood.

One remembers too, of course, the ones that 'got away', notably an eighteenth-century house with a cupola, which sold for the £40 I could not afford. There was also the strange house with its long passage at the back, from which doors opened into rooms facing the spectator. Years later I believe I met it again, furnished, touchingly I thought, with a good many sequins, silver card and artefacts of mother-of-pearl. It is now in a display at a great country house. I longed for that one, for I only once had seen the same architecture in a family house, Clare Hall, now in a museum in Suffolk.

It seemed that dolls' houses might be found where the pine trees grew, and certainly Malmö at that time (the 1950s) was more rewarding than Paris. Although greatly flattered to find my recently published book in the museum library, I was more delighted to realize that it must have been bought because of an earlier interest in the subject. Later – and it was one of those small discoveries that are so delightful to the researcher – the splendid museum in Stockholm showed Waltershausen furniture made with Scandinavian taste in mind – that is, 'rosewood' treated to resemble pale birchwood or in white.

Another such pleasure was when, having looked closely at hundreds of desks, dressing-tables and other pieces of furniture, I asked doubtfully what was the substance from which the delicate white supporting pillars were made – bone, perhaps, or some fine-grained local wood? 'Elefantbein', I was assured. But surely not, not for toys sold for pennies in England. Yes, it was ivory. And then I remembered the great piano manufacturing centres – Bluthner at Leipzig or, further, Steinway at Hamburg – and how the shards must fall when the keys were cut. A quite plausible explanation, certainly in the early days of manufacture.

These are the sparkles in the sand that reward the researcher and the collector.

VIVIEN GREENE

WILLIAM
AND MARY

LATE SEVENTEENTH OR EARLY EIGHTEENTH CENTURY

Height	*38 1/2in*	*(98cm)*
Width	*23 1/2in*	*(60cm)*
Depth	*14in*	*(35cm)*

T HIS HOUSE is a simple cupboard in straight-grained oak, with quoining down the sides, a plain cornice (part of which is missing) and a glazed door. The type is characteristic of the early English houses under Dutch influence. The interior has three shelves, providing four rooms, each with a corner fireplace. These fireplaces are common in late seventeenth-century houses influenced by Dutch examples and are usually found in small rooms or closets; some have shelves for the display of Chinese porcelain or Delft. In his diary, I believe, Samuel Pepys mentions them as an innovation.

The rooms in plain wood, are undecorated and have been left unfurnished. They are: top room, with a square fireplace opening, unmoulded, with no skirtings; second-floor room, with a moulded opening to the square fireplace, skirtings and cornice; first-floor room, the main room of the house, with a more elaborately moulded fireplace, skirtings, cornice and a moulded panel above the fireplace for a painting or mirror to be inserted, a feature of early houses that recurs in the later Van Haeften House (see pages 33–5); ground-floor room, no doubt the kitchen, with no skirtings or cornice, but the fireplace opening has an arched top.

PORTOBELLO

1700–10

Height	*48in*	*(122cm)*
Width	*54 1/2in*	*(138cm)*
Depth	*21 1/2in*	*(55cm)*

THIS HOUSE IS MADE OF OAK, as is the cabinet of Ann Sharp's baby house of the 1690s, which belongs to the Bulwer Long family and is the most perfectly preserved early house. This example is a little later, perhaps about 1700–1710, and it is a house, not a cabinet. Very little furniture of this date is extant and the house is furnished mainly with late eighteenth-century and early nineteenth-century pieces.

This house, which stood unsold for a long time in London's Portobello Road street market, was later owned by Charles Forte – not the well-respected hotelier, but an elderly antiques dealer who lived in a cottage near Worthing. The baby house was not part of his stock but his private treasure, and it stood in his kitchen at the back of the one-room shop. It must have been late in the evening when I arrived by appointment to draw and measure the huge early eighteenth-century structure. One candle stood on his kitchen table, which was neatly covered in newspaper, and another was in his hand as he showed me the 'sliding cheek' of the kitchen grate, a device by which an eighteenth-century cook was able to reduce the size of the fire for economy. There was not much furniture in the baby house, but I vividly remember the many oil paintings in colour on the parlour walls, and also in the parlour a tiny ivory model, rigging and all, of a sailing ship. There was a set of Chinese 'rice' porcelain dishes, 1in (2.5cm) long, where small holes in the paste in the shape of rice grains are covered by translucent glaze. There were six dish-covers in the kitchen, a clock and early earthenware plates and dishes, all seen by candlelight, producing a sense almost of awe at the age and, one could say, personality of the structure. Years later Mr Forte, then on his deathbed, told his niece, 'Let Mrs Greene have it, she has some sense.'

The kitchen. The extraordinary adjustable kitchen grate is of wrought steel and the central basket for the fire can be narrowed or widened by means of ratchets, worked by keys (now missing) at either side. It must have been made by an experienced smith, as it is a working model. The fact that there are hobs on each side indicates that it may be rather later than the house, as this type of grate was not common before the middle of the eighteenth century. The furniture, which is very simple, includes a high shelf for pans, a dresser and a table. There are a lot of tinplate items: a painted toast-rack, the set of dish-covers, a candle box on the rear wall, a cheese grater, a hastener without a jack and a tinderbox. A copper warming pan hangs on the wall; the copper pans are modern. The wax jack (above) is rare in miniature, with its neat device for holding a length of taper, which then was melted and dripped on a letter to seal it; these, made in brass, were in use from the seventeenth century. With it is the tinplate candle box, open to show the candles, and a basket of oysters.

The front is made in three removable sections: a centre panel with the front door and two side wings, each with a lock. The windows, with their six panes, appear to be casements, a style which gave way rapidly in the early eighteenth century to sashes, so that few eighteenth-century houses with their casements survive, most having been replaced. The keystones over the windows are also an early feature. The door casing is a version of the style made popular by the Baroque architect James Gibbs.

The interior is interestingly asymmetrical, like some Dutch houses, with four rooms and an entrance hall. The staircase leads from the hall up to a landing with a small arch, but does not, for some reason, return to the first floor behind its wall. The left-hand room upstairs has a door in the wall leading to a small boxed-in area where the landing should be. The hall has a storage area under the staircase. There is also a working back door in the kitchen, painted dark green. The interior is unpainted and unpapered, just a plain mellow oak. The cabinetwork is very neat and plain; the doors are not panelled but have elaborate brass hinges and handles.

The dining room. The principal feature of this room is the built-in corner cabinet, the upper part glazed and with elaborate brass butterfly hinges, containing porcelain, the lower part with a solid door. Corner fittings, fire places and cupboards were typical of early houses, as we have seen in the William and Mary cabinet (see pages 18–19), probably under Dutch influence. The fireplace, of the type called a Forest grate, is a later cast-iron chimney ornament. The early fire-irons are brass, and the bellows are covered in red leather. There is a set of eighteenth-century chairs in thin mahogany, perhaps home-made, and a later drop-leaf table made from a cigar box marked 'Flor de Sumatra'. In the corner is a later long-case clock. The blue and white is Staffordshire pottery and Chinese porcelain.

The parlour. The free-standing fireplace is of enamelled tinplate, early nineteenth century in date and most unusual, with its hand-painted or stencilled decorations. Beside it sits an elderly man with a cello, in a home-made Georgian armchair covered in silk, with pins acting as upholstery nails all round the edge. The rest of the furniture is later, including an English mahogany pedestal table of about 1860, on which stands a miniature silver coffee-pot, a candlestick and so on. Note also the Chinese porcelain vases on the mantelpiece and table.

The parlour. The room is painted a distressed green. The piecrust table and chair are mid-eighteenth century. In the corner hangs a cupboard with mirror glass doors, identical to another in the Mahogany House (see pages 27–9). A fine Georgian miniature tallboy stands by the window. An eighteenth-century silver coffee-pot is on the table, and miniature Chinese porcelain vases are on the shelves. The door in the corner leads to the inaccessible landing.

Exterior. The façade is fixed, but the front door opens, as do wings on each of the side walls. The roof is sunk behind the cornice, with two oblong chimneys. The façade is painted brick, with heavy quoining painted in a stippled technique. The windows have heavy mouldings and the door has a pedimented surround. Inside, there are two rooms on each side, and a hall, stairs and landing in the centre are visible through the side rooms or through the open front door.

THE GEORGIAN HOUSE

1720–30

Height   37in   (94cm) excluding stand
Width   35½in (90cm)
Depth   20in   (51cm)

T HIS IS A TYPICAL small early Georgian house of the kind found in country towns and is made of oak. This house was called 'The Haunted House' in my first book, in which I described the labours long ago of removing cement and enamel paint from all the surfaces, and the addition of pillars in the opening between the right-hand room and the hall; I would not have made such an alteration at a later date. The furniture, which has been added, is mainly early – i.e. of the late eighteenth and early nineteenth centuries – with a few home-made pieces. When the house first came to me, our fantasy was that it was haunted, and a ghost was provided that gibbered in the parlour, with a clockwork mechanism. The house was exhibited at the first major dolls'-house exhibition, at the House of Bewlay in Park Lane, which opened in November 1955. I was told that the young Prince Charles visited and said, 'Make the ghost work', but they couldn't operate the mechanism!

The dining parlour. The walls and the added marbled pillars are painted green, and between the pillars is seen the oak staircase, which turns into the dark upstairs landing. On the floor is a copper wine cooler with two bottles. There is an early chair, and a pedestal table which holds a candlestick, snuffer and a silver wine funnel. The Bijou Bible, published by Rock Bros and Payne, is inscribed 'Jenny' on the flyleaf; it is abridged for children.

The kitchen. The paintwork is eggshell blue. In the deep fireplace is a later tin range with opening hob doors. In front of the fire is a large tin plate-warmer and hanging from the mantelshelf is a clockwork jack. In the early Georgian period in a small house like this, there would probably have been a free-standing fire grate, with pots hanging over it from a chimney crane. The tall dresser has an array of pewter, a copper kettle is on the fender, and a grill hangs on the wall. Hanging on the right is a wooden birdcage.

The bedroom. The walls are painted peacock green, with red brocade curtains, and the fireplace has a marbled surround. I made the bed from two fan handles and embroidered Chinese silk. There is a small triangular washstand and a Dutch mahogany chest of drawers with ivory knobs. On this is an eighteenth-century silver chamber candlestick and a rare ivory wig-stand. I envisaged the house as occupied by an old miser, so a trunk with coins is kept at the foot of the bed.

THE
MAHOGANY HOUSE

1730–40

Height   *50½in*   *(128cm)*   *including stand*
Width   *31in*   *(79cm)*
Depth   *15½in*   *(39cm)*

This was made in the period of transition from the cabinet on a stand to the house on a stand. The mahogany house sits on its original stand, which is very tall and slim. The centre panel in front is fixed, although the front door opens. There are no chimneys, and the flat roof opens, having a lock and handle. The two side wings have both locks and turn-buttons. The glazed window in the front, and the two windows on each side, have nicely detailed mouldings, as does the doorcase. The six-panel front door has the panels defined by inlaid bands of two woods. Beside the front door is the bell-pull, which has a wire and a working bell. The whole design is a mixture of the eccentricity and attention to detail typical of very early houses.

The doors are a dull white, and the walls, except the kitchen, are painted in shades of blue. The fireplace surrounds are flatly moulded and lightly marbled. Because of the age of the house, furniture of the period is not obtainable, so much of the contents are modern reproduction. Despite this, the house retains a strong sense of the past, full of character and originality.

The parlour. The room is painted blue, with a white dado and green skirting. Above the white marbled fireplace is the remains of a gilt mirror painted on the wall, most happily rescued when papers were removed. A small miniature portrait hangs at one side. The pedestal table is German.

The hall. The winding staircase at the back of the hall seems to lead to the landing, the latter being actually accessible only from the opening roof. In fact, the staircase stops at the first turn, being made as a separate unit which can be lifted out. The section of staircase appearing on the landing is also separate. The hall and landing have opening doors to each room. A most interesting feature, similar to certain Dutch houses, is the painted dummy cabinet door beside the staircase, beneath which is a real 'cupboard under the stairs'. The floor is marked out in diamond-shaped flagstones.

The kitchen. The room is painted in a faded celadon green, above brown skirting. The floor is painted with diamond-shaped red tiles. The fireplace, corner shelves and another shelf to the left was built in. In the corner hangs the front doorbell. Some kitchen equipment has been added: an Evans and Cartwright stove, a pestle and mortar, and a rare tinplate tinder box on the table. An early (late eighteenth-century) toy clock hangs on the wall in painted wood, its maker inscribed as 'Bosher, London'. There is no known clockmaker of this name, so it was perhaps the toymaker's bid for immortality. There is a table which must be by the same maker, with a similar naïve painted trailing pattern, in Marble Hall (see pages 69–71).

QUANTOCK OAK

1730–40

Height	*66 ¹/₂in*	*(169cm)*	*including the original oak stand*
Width	*48in*	*(122cm)*	
Depth	*20 ¹/₂in*	*(52cm)*	

I VISITED AN IMMENSE HOUSE in Somerset, which was occupied by my hostess and her two daughters, who had suggested that I stay overnight to see their three dolls' houses. One, I think, was modern; another charming house dated from the early years of this century and the third was totally breathtaking. It was oak and therefore very early eighteenth century – say, 1730 perhaps – with a splendid staircase and hall floor inlaid with a pattern which I thought confirmed an early date. My hostess complained that it took up too much room, though I remarked on her eight empty bedrooms. Never in my travels have I hinted at a longing to acquire a possession so kindly shown at my request – to do so would be an insult coming from a guest – but here, such a happy ending. About five years later a letter came saying that their home was too big for their family and, having noticed my rapture for the big dolls' house, would I like to add it to the collection. The only fact they knew about it was that it had been bought some years earlier from a dealer in the Quantocks.

This grand Palladian oak house was clearly, if not an adaptation of a real house, professionally designed using the architectural manuals of the period. It bears some similarities to the work of John Wood the Elder, the architect of Queen Square in Bath. The house is constructed on a heavily rusticated base, in which at that period it was proper to house 'cellars, kitchens, woodhouses, bakehouses, storerooms, laundries, and other offices, which might with advantage be partly underground', as then 'the body of the house will be more ample, commodious, healthy and pleasant'. In the baby house it becomes a store or toy cupboard. Above the base is a rusticated ground floor containing the kitchen etc., and above that the *piano nobile*. The rustication consists of bevelled 1-in (2.5-cm) square oak tiles, iron-hard, glued to the structure. There are windows at the side as well as in front, two for each room except the kitchen.

The upper hall. This has a neoclassical paper frieze of paired gryphons facing urns, and portrait prints, *c.* 1800.

The house has a most complex system of opening, whereby a hand must be inserted through the front door after unlocking it, so that a hidden bolt can be drawn before the front section can be opened and the two side wings operated. It would indeed be difficult for a naughty child to burgle! Inside we enter a central hall, with a kitchen on the right and another room to the left. Stairs climb to the principal floor, where the ceilings are a third higher than downstairs. At this period the principal floor of a great house comprised rooms of 'taste, expense, state, and parade' and perhaps the rooms here were originally intended as an antechamber, a saloon and a state bedroom. The family in such a house, when not entertaining, sometimes lived in cosier rooms in 'the rustick' – that is, the lower floor. All the rooms are now furnished with a set of over-large scale mahogany pieces, English, of about 1860; they are broadly similar to the large-scale furniture in Mrs Bryant's house in the Museum of Childhood at Bethnal Green, London.

This room has a fireplace similar to the kitchen, but beside it is an alcove with an arched top. On the side wall are two built-in storage boxes, which can serve as seats, and a table supported on two brackets. It is not clear whether this room would have been used as a pantry or a parlour, or whether it was a servants' or housekeeper's room.

VAN HAEFTEN
HOUSE

1740–50

Height	*49in*	*(124cm)*
Width	*50in*	*(127cm)*
Depth	*19in*	*(48cm)*

T HIS BEAUTIFUL, ruinous house was acquired in 1966 from Baroness Ann
van Haeften. She told me that in 1885 her mother, as a child, had saved
her pocket money and done jobs in the garden to be able to buy the
house from a second-hand shop in Hawkhurst, Kent. The house moved with her
to Scotland, then to London during the First World War and finally, during the
Second World War, was sent to the Baroness as the eldest daughter. There was
never any furniture, although she and her sister had made some of cardboard
when they were young.

When it arrived, many pieces of moulding, inside and out, and all the glazing bars except for one window were missing. The repairs executed in 1967 by a modern craftsman, Mr Peter Baker, are shown unpainted and undisguised for comparison with the original work, to which they are quite equal in delicacy and skill.

The exterior is that of a Palladian mansion, finely proportioned, standing on an original arcaded base. It was not unusual for Georgian buildings to be raised on heavily rusticated arched bases, to cope with changes of level or service areas, although here, of course, it is done simply to raise the house from the floor. The coat of drab paint was on the house when aquired, although a scrape of the pediment showed that at one time the house was covered in small brickwork, some of which remains.

The interior has been left unfurnished. It is empty to show the panelling better, and also because contemporary furniture is not available. The two visiting dolls are being shown round by a house agent. The kitchen has built-in shelves and a rack for spits over the fireplace, and all the other rooms have fine chimney-pieces. Details of the ground floor and staircase show the quality of the construction. In two rooms the original overmantel pictures, in their built-in frames, survive. The ground-floor painting is an oil showing hounds in the foreground of an Italianate landscape with a huntsman; the one upstairs shows cattle in a Continental landscape. This treatment of pictures as part of the decoration rather than as separate objects was quite usual in the eighteenth century, although as John Cornforth remarks in his book *English Decoration in the Eighteenth Century:* 'In most cases the pictures were only of moderate quality, being vaguely classical landscapes, ruin pieces, or sets of lesser relations by minor painters.' In the case of a baby house, we should not jib at the quality; it is amazing to have them at all.

Overmantel painting, ground floor

BELOW LEFT: Ground Floor detail.

BELOW: Staircase detail.

The façade is that of a substantial Palladian country mansion, with heavy pilasters and a rusticated basement floor. The front steps are missing. The green marbling on the pilasters is original, although a little restored.

The settee, which has its arms missing, and matching chairs are of wood. The seats are carved to imitate rush, with wire stretchers, and are painted red with yellow markings to imitate the kind of mock-bamboo furniture popular in the Regency period, when the chinoiserie style favoured by the Prince was at its height. This type of furniture, also found in yellow, is rare and English, but the manufacturer is unknown.

THE
GREAT HOUSE

circa 1750

Height	*63 ¹/₂in*	*(161cm)* *excluding modern stand*
Width	*71in*	*(180cm)*
Depth	*20 ¹/₂in*	*(52cm)*

MANY YEARS AGO my daughter wrote from York that a charity exhibition there was showing 'a huge dolls' house'. But by then the exhibition had closed and the owner of the house could not be traced. However, quite by accident I was directed to the Deramore family, who also had a dolls' house, and so I wrote to Lady Deramore, asking whether I might call to measure and photograph it. At that time film was almost impossible to buy and I invariably found a village photographer, accustomed to taking photographs of footballers or wedding parties, to do a 'passport' photograph of the house, to look at and learn from before any repairs were done or furnishing was introduced. Somehow, I cannot remember how, the letter of permission directed me to a factor, or agent, who met me at a vast eighteenth-century house, vacant for some years, on a hill in the Yorkshire countryside. There I was taken to a large garage or stables, containing a very old damaged car, a bicycle or two, and a splendid baby house, with a flight of steps to a pedimented door on the *piano nobile*.

Very soon afterwards 'the Great House', almost identical to the Yorkshire house, appeared in Gloucestershire, with the pediment missing but the same pilasters on each side. The pediment was easily copied from the Yorkshire house by a cabinet-maker. The Great House is a fine example of the English eighteenth-century habit of providing a magnificent architectural housing for what is essentially a simple four-room dwelling. This contrasts with the Dutch tradition of fitting elaborate rooms into cabinets with little or no resemblance to a house. Dating from around 1750, the origins of this Palladian house are unknown, but it is believed to have come originally from Cheshire or Lancashire. When the house was found the outside was thickly coated in chocolate paint and the inside with many layers of wallpaper, which, as so often, required hours of work with fingernails, broken glass

The front door and window above are on a fixed panel, with an opening wing on each side. The rooms do, however, have doors into the central staircase area. The staircase – wide enough for one of my Burmese cats to ascend – leads up to a green-painted landing. At the bottom of the stairs is a curtail step – that is, it has a curved end projecting outwards. The hall is also painted dull green and has an arch with a keystone leading to a rear area. The scale of the rooms is large, rather over 1:12, but this is exaggerated by the high ceilings, especially on the upper (*piano nobile*) floor.

and other methods. Originally the whole house except the kitchen had been painted a deep peacock blue, with a line marking the wainscot. The proportions are excellent, the maker having provided a false basement floor for service rooms to make the façade convincing architecturally, although inside the kitchen is on the ground floor, most unlikely in a real house at this period. One chimney and the pediment have had to be replaced, as described above, and the stand is modern. No furniture remained; since furniture of the early eighteenth century is very rare, most of the 'new' pieces are late eighteenth or early nineteenth century.

The drawing room. On the first floor and painted blue, this contains a fine early nineteenth-century mahogany miniature bookcase and a mahogany chest of drawers. There is a handsome early brass grate in the original chimney-piece.

The kitchen. This room has a fine tinplate stove for cooking (later than the probable date of the house) and a brick copper on one side. Coppers, which are found in both kitchens and sculleries of old houses, were used not only for heating water for laundry but also for boiling hams and for brewing beer; as late as 1845 Mrs Loudon, in The Lady's Country Companion, describes these tedious processes. In front of the stove stands a tinplate hastener with a clockwork bottle jack. Other tinplate items include a salt box, a turquoise pail and a gravy drainer. On the shelf against the rear wall are two pointed sugar loaves, painted blue as they were always wrapped in blue paper. On the mantelpiece are two late eighteenth-century dishes from a toy dinner service.

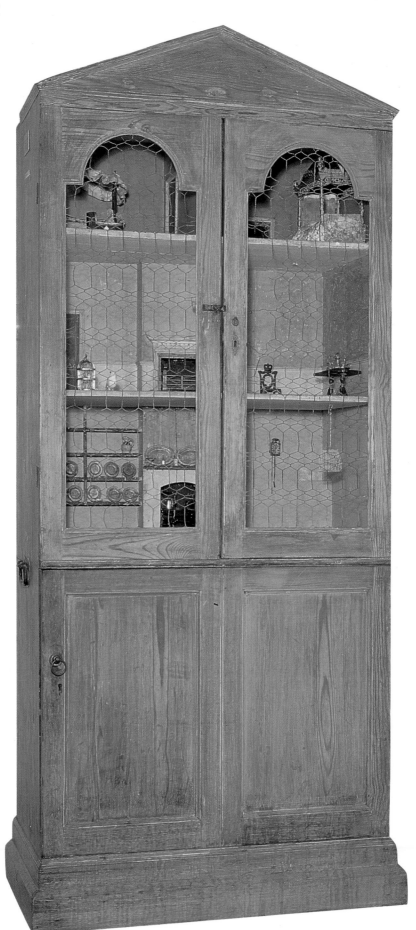

The cabinet is made of
stained pine, which may
originally have been
painted. There are heavy
carrying handles on the
sides; the cabinet is
made in two sections.
The brass-wire grille is
original but rather
fragile. The toy
cupboard underneath
has a shaped shelf, as if a
small toy horse might
have been stabled there.

THE
WIRE CABINET

MID-EIGHTEENTH CENTURY

Height   76 ¹/₂in   *(194cm)*   *including cupboard base*
Width   32in   *(81cm)*
Depth   18 ¹/₂in   *(47cm)*

THIS INTERESTING CABINET, which houses both a toy cupboard and a dolls' house, probably dates from the reign of George II. It was bought in the 1970s by my friend Faith Rowntree from an antiques dealer in Lincoln. It came to the collection in 1977, when it was auctioned at Sotheby's. I removed modern wallpapers.

Interior There are four rooms, the top shelf being divided into two bedrooms. The wall between the two rooms has a non-opening door. The floors are bare, and the walls are painted a stone colour. There is a fire surround in the right-hand room, but the fireplace is simply painted as a black square. A modern four-poster has been put in each room. The middle floor is the saloon. The walls are covered with old paper above a chair rail, and there is a dummy door, with a moulded door case, in the rear wall. The kitchen fills the bottom floor. It has a bare wood floor and a moulded, white-painted fireplace, containing a nineteenth-century tinplate kitchen grate with bars, hobs and a fender. A set of German pewter plates stands on built-in shelves.

41

The front façade of the house is in three sections. The centre portion has two locks, hidden normally by movable sections of the string course, and a locking front door. When a small ring is used to pull open the centre section, the left-hand door can then be opened. The pediment has a neoclassical fan-shaped ornament.

CANE END HOUSE

circa 1760

Height	*57in*	*(145cm)*
Width	*61in*	*(155cm)*
Depth	*20in*	*(51cm)*

THIS BABY HOUSE belonged to the Vanderstegen family of Cane End House, in the parish of Kidmore End near Reading, until the death of the last member in 1940. Cane End was originally Canons' End, a house belonging to the abbot and Augustinian canons of Netley Abbey. On the dissolution of the monasteries by Henry VIII, the house was bought by Sir Anthony Brigham, cofferer to his majesty, and in 1759 a descendant of his, Elizabeth Brigham, married William Vanderstegen, whose father had come from Holland with William III. It seems likely that the baby house dates from shortly after this marriage. Reputedly, the baby house was designed in the Chippendale workshops, and the master copied for it in miniature the furniture he had designed for the family. Cane End itself had been rebuilt in 1704 and I had hoped that the baby house was that very rare thing, a replica of the owner's real house, but the two are far from identical.

The baby house was eventually sold at Christie's by Douglas Vanderstegen in the 1930s for 120 guineas, described as having '6 rooms, a fine winding staircase, Chippendale furniture and figures in costume'. Sadly, the Chinese Chippendale furniture and the dolls were dispersed at some time after the sale. The only record I have is a picture from the *Reading Mercury*, 28 November 1925, showing the original toy furniture, including a set of Chippendale-type dining chairs. The following quotation from the *Daily Mail* casts some light on the family's situation in the 1930s; it relates to the Ideal Home Exhibition, for which Vanderstegen items were being lent:

Mr Douglas Vanderstegen, bachelor scion of a line that came to England with William of Orange, was showing a vast hoard of clothes, trinkets, diaries, and furniture, an accumulated legacy since 1786 . . . Great-grandmother Vanderstegen kept a diary from 1758–9 . . . items included Chippendale card tables from the workshop of the young master.

The baby house had a chequered career. At the Christie's auction it was bought in by the last surviving member of the Vanderstegen family, and when he died in 1940 Cane End House itself was sold, and all its contents. The baby house then seems to have passed through several hands, including auctions. After more than two years, having had tantalizing bits of information about it, I eventually tracked it down to a firm of antique dealers. By this time not only had all the contents disappeared but garish enamel paint covered the exterior, the floors and doors had been painted black and the early wood-block wallpapers covered with modern paper.

The windows and fanlight are all nicely moulded, and the centre front has decorative quoining.

The photograph shows most effectively the sweeping curves of the mahogany staircase, which is the greatest beauty of this house. Doors open on the three landings to six rooms, the doors being six-panelled on their outer sides but two-panelled on the inside and of the low, wide, Georgian proportions. Most of them have small brass open drop handles. In each room, on the outside wall, is another door opposite the first one which is false. These false doors could indicate closets, or they could be a reflection of the Georgian practice of creating enfilades of rooms, each with a view into the next, so that when all the doors are open a splendid vista appeared. The doorcases and the fireplaces are all moulded.

The kitchen. This very satisfactory working kitchen has whitewashed walls and a floor which I marked with large grey flagstones. There is a large built-in dresser, and the fireplace has a spit rack and a rare smoke jack, a mechanism by which in real life a fan driven by the rising air in the chimney worked a spit by means of chains. Part of the mechanism can be seen on the near side of the fireplace. In front of the fire a small doll is making a piece of toast on a long fork. There is a pair of brass scales on the rear wall, and plenty of other equipment, including a chestnut roaster, pans and moulds. On the dresser at the back is a turned wooden dinner service from Saxony, decorated with flowers and including jugs, coffeepot, basin, vase, etc. Another doll is about to prepare a large goose whose neck hangs over the table edge.

CANE END HOUSE

The landing. Here stands a black page which I made and dressed in a blue uniform, trimmed with silver lace. The elegant cantilevered staircase curves upwards, its balusters being brass rods and the handrail ending in a carved spiral. The green early hand-blocked wallpaper has stripes of formalized flowers in white and a zigzag border. This wallpaper, with its fresh design based on textile patterns of the period, was probably intended for a small parlour or bedroom of a real house.

The bedroom. Papered with another green and white early print, this room has no dado. The wallpaper has a pattern of white wreaths with ears of corn in their centre, with a neoclassical effect. There are two rugs, one being a piece of red brocade. A four-poster in mahogany has early cotton hangings and a gold embroidered bedspread. The chest of drawers is a model which does not open. On the late Georgian washstand is a silver jug and basin. A good miniature mirror stands on the dressing table. By the bed is a gilt metal hanging shelf with two small basins. By the fireplace on a trivet stands a miniature silver posset-pot, intended for serving warm drinks at bedtime or for an invalid.

The dining room. The wallpaper is the same as in the drawing room, but here it is combined with blue paintwork on the dado and so on. The fireplace is marbled a dark blue and the chandelier is glass. Under the dining table is a woolwork rug. The small settee and two Waltershausen chairs are covered in red brocade. On the dining table is a ribbed glass decanter with the remains of wine in it, two air-twist glasses and two smaller glasses. There is a nineteenth-century gilt brass birdcage on a stand. A mahogany built-in shelf on the right side acts as a serving table.

The drawing room. This has a splendid block-printed eighteenth-century wallpaper, in this case a pink ground with stripes decorated with formalized green leaves. At the ceiling and dado are matching borders with a zigzag design, and the dado and doors are white. The furniture includes a fine miniature double chest of drawers and an early nineteenth-century toy square piano with an 'Andante' ready to be performed. The settee and small chairs of Georgian style I recovered in a silk brocade rescued from Bowood House when it was partly demolished; the red fabric hanging in shreds from the walls had partly fallen on the floor. There is a folding card table, on which lie a heap of toy playing cards. An early round picture has a female portrait in a surround of tinsel of various colours. The marbled mantelpiece has pots of flowers in glass, and a glass chandelier hangs from the ceiling. The carpet is woolwork.

THE TRAVELLING BABY HOUSE

EIGHTEENTH CENTURY

Height 17½in (44cm)
Width 10½in (26cm)
Depth 15½in (25cm)

THIS LITTLE HOUSE is in mahogany, the front opening in one wing with a catch at the side. The façade has its original diamond inlay of ivory and mother-of-pearl. On top at each side are brass balls. One of the fixings for side handles remains, in brass, in the shape of a lion's head.

The windows are glass, with green curtains painted on the inside. The interior has two rooms, each with a fireplace; they would have had free-standing fire dogs or grates. The dados are plain wood, with green paint above. Scorch marks on the ceilings show where candles have been used; perhaps the house was once illuminated as a night-light.

In *Gulliver's Travels*, published in 1726, the giant Princess of Brobdingnag keeps the captured Gulliver in a travelling house which she takes in her coach as a child might take a pet mouse. Gulliver describes the furnishing of the house:

> a nice workman who was famous for little curiosities undertook to make me two chairs and two tables with a cabinet to put my things in . . . I had an entire set of silver dishes and plates, which in proportion to those of the Queen's was not bigger than what I have seen of the same kind in a London toyshop for the furniture of a baby house.

It would be wonderful if the furniture of this house had survived.

Exterior.

49

THE
DOWER HOUSE

MID-EIGHTEENTH CENTURY

Height	*27in*	*(69cm)*
Width	*37½in*	*(95cm)*
Depth	*22½in*	*(57cm)*

T HIS ELEGANT LITTLE MID-EIGHTEENTH-CENTURY HOUSE has no history. All the furniture has been added. As eighteenth-century toy furniture is so scarce, I have furnished it as it might have been in 1860–70.

The house, which is painted pale fawn, has a Baroque stand with fierce carved birds as supports, (This is not original.) The six-panelled front door opens, and the house front opens in two wings, with small urn finials on top. The roof is flat and there are two thin chimneys. There are also four side windows. At the left-hand side is a four-panelled kitchen door in a nicely moulded case, and a window with an arched top (left), through which the cook can be seen taking a short rest from her labours.

Inside are four rooms, and a hall and landing with rather narrow stairs for the Georgian period. All the rooms are painted in plain colours; it is not known if this is original.

The drawing room. This pink room has a patterned needlework carpet with a fringe. Two boys in sailor suits are with their grandmother, and the nursemaid holds a baby. In the background a girl practises at the pianoforte. The furniture is mainly Waltershausen; chairs, sofa, piano, sewing table and a table with a transfer decoration of a river scene. A gilt pendulum clock is on the mantelpiece. The table with the potted plant has a beaded top.

52

OVERLEAF: **The kitchen.** The stove is Evans and Cartwright, with the usual arrangement of the hot-water boiler and the oven on each side of the fire. On it sits a shining copper kettle. Above on the wall are two tin plates embossed with fish. A brass birdcage hangs at the window. The table and plate rack are old, and the dresser and chair modern. The tinplate mangle in a traditional shape is by the British firm of Holdfast and dates from the twentieth century.

The bedroom. In this blue room, on a flowered woolwork carpet, a sombrely clad bisque mother addresses a young daughter (who is an early doll of about 1840, with a papier mâché head on a wooden body and a striped silk dress). The curtains are in early cotton print. Over the fireplace hangs a tiny original sampler, signed and dated 'M.A.W. Clarke, 1800'. There are views of the Crystal Palace in an oval frame, and of Chillon Castle, popular because of a poem by Byron. The furniture includes a Waltershausen dressing table (left), in the mixed Gothic/Louis style, fashionable around 1850, and a tinplate washstand with holes for bottles, bowl, etc. The chest at the left is English. The later gilt metal bed is surmounted with eagles.

The dining room. The walls are green, and red Turkey carpet is under the table. On the mantelpiece is a Waltershausen clock and two milk glass vases. On a plinth is a head of Apollo, similar to one in my own dining room. There are many pictures, and a gilt mirror with a candle sconce. A bisque lady and gentleman face each other challengingly, as in a Compton-Burnett novel.

The four-panelled kitchen door and arched window at the left-hand side.

THE

RICHARDSON HOUSE

MID-EIGHTEENTH CENTURY

Height 42in (107cm) excluding stand
Width 36in (91cm)
Depth 15in (38cm)

THIS HOUSE WAS BOUGHT by the late Sir Albert Richardson, past president of the Royal Academy and pre-eminent authority on eighteenth-century architecture, and donated by his grandson Simon Houfe. The magnificent wallpaper in the drawing room was identified by Mr Abbott Lowell Cummings, Assistant Director of the Fogg Art Museum, Mass., USA, who told me that he had a piece of this paper in his files dated 1777. The mid-Victorian furniture, most of it Waltershausen, was in the house. Wallpaper in the other rooms was in poor condition and has been replaced with modern papers.

The kitchen. This is papered in the traditional blue. The fireplace has a marbled surround, with a fine Evans and Cartwright stove, with the typical pressed tinplate mouldings on the top at the rear; the gilt tap is from the hot-water boiler. If this were an original fitting, the date of the house would need to be reconsidered. A built-in plate rack has a slightly splashed painted finish. A dresser top is fixed to the right wall, and a small pine dresser stands on the left. The equipment includes a tinplate kettle, a painted hot-water can and a red hanging tinplate box, probably for salt.

The roof is shallow-pitched, behind a cornice. The front façade, which is not shown, is very plain, with glazed windows lacking glazing bars, opening in two wings. The house has six rooms, two of which are attics, and a hall, stairs and first-floor landing. The stairs to the attic lead into the right-hand room. The interior woodwork is marbled green and white.

The dining room. I have repapered this in an early nineteenth-century style. The extending imitation rosewood dining table, chairs, cabinet with shelves above and dressing table used as a sideboard are Waltershausen. A low vitrine is in the German mottled-brown wood finish, contemporary with Waltershausen but of a less perfect manufacture.

The drawing room. This has a striking appearance, with apparently two different old wallpapers, one with birds like pheasants and the other with large roses in leaves. The needlework carpet is an aggressive green and black. The Waltershausen rosewood furniture includes a Biedermeier sofa and cabinet, and a Gothic revival cabinet. At the back is a Waltershausen secretaire in light wood. The fireplace is marbled, with a brass fender.

THE

BALUSTRADED HOUSE

circa 1775

Height	*62 ¹/₂in*	*(159cm)*	*including the original arcaded stand*
Width	*57in*	*(145cm)*	
Depth	*20 ¹/₂in*	*(52cm)*	

T HIS BEAUTIFUL HOUSE has no ascertainable history (in my first book it was named 'Mid-Georgian 3'). It had no furniture and is largely furnished with modern miniature reproductions or mid-nineteenth-century pieces.

The house has an extremely well-designed, elaborate exterior, sitting nicely on the heavy arches of its original stand, which has some similarity to the stand of the Uppark baby house. The front is scored as stone only below the string course, and the rest is brickwork. The balusters of the top balustrade are turned wood. On each side of the house are six glazed windows, not visible in the picture; four of them on each side have been blacked out with pitch, to avoid the window tax which was imposed originally in 1697, and later much increased, not being repealed until 1851. The opening double front door, with its small porch, supports a tiny balcony with wire railings.

The front of the house opens in three wings, showing each of the rooms framed in a curved proscenium, a rather unusual feature. There are three floors, six rooms, a staircase with a central hall and two landings. The staircase, finely modelled, has brass wire banisters (late Georgian houses had plainer, more spindly features than early ones). The hall has an old marbled paper floor marked out with tiles. The house was painted inside, and the original paintwork survives in four rooms, having been restored elsewhere. The curtains have been made in eighteenth-century fabrics. All the rooms have neat hob grates with an impressed neoclassical pattern.

The dining room. This room, which has a side window and two doors, is painted a vivid peacock blue and has a paisley carpet. At the back of the room is a curtain of old printed chintz, covering an arched recess. On the left are two six-panelled doors, one leading to the hall and the other being false. All the furniture except for the centre pedestal table is modern miniature.

The kitchen. As is usual, this room is painted blue to discourage flies. An old tinplate stove, probably by Evans and Cartwright, has been added (left). This type of stove, manufactured in cast iron, became popular for kitchens in the early nineteenth century, replacing the hob grate. It provided for hot water to be heated on the left side by heat from the central fire, and for other food to be baked in the oven to the right. Although the oven heating was uneven, and the massive cast iron radiated heat wastefully, stoves like this were used for a very long period, despite the fact that as early as 1830 gas-fired stoves were being produced. On the right side by the fire can be seen the hole in the floor where originally the weight from the spit, unwinding on its chain, descended. There is a spit rack, but no mechanism remains. There are some pieces of old tinplate, including a small Dutch oven and a shovel. A hedgehog trots across the floor; they were sometimes kept in kitchens to eat up the blackbeetles. At the back of the room are coops with a few chickens; these also were often kept for a short time in the kitchen, to be fattened up on the scraps before being killed. This was also a German practice and coops can be seen in Nuremberg toy kitchens. On the kitchen table there is a model of a salmagundi, which I took from a 1780 cookery book. The recipe ordered boiled herrings, cooked chicken and hard-boiled eggs to be put in layers in a mould: 'Finally decorate with the fish bones.'

THE
HASKELL HOUSE

LATE EIGHTEENTH CENTURY

Height	*33 ¹/₂in*	*(85cm)*	
Width	*26 ¹/₂in*	*(67cm)*	*at base*
Depth	*14 ¹/₂in*	*(36cm)*	*including base*

THIS SMALL EIGHTEENTH-CENTURY house is one of two generously presented by Sir Arnold Haskell, who arrived one afternoon out of the blue. It was decorated by his mother in the mid-1920s. Mrs Haskell made all the furniture, the curtains, etc., and this house was reminiscent of her own home in Bath. The exquisite detail is all her own work. A third dolls' house was presented to the London Museum when it was housed in Lancaster House. The style of lighting dates from the 1920s and has been left unchanged, although modern miniature lighting is less obtrusive. The decor is a realization of a distinctive but short-lived style which has been pinned down for ever by Osbert Lancaster as 'Curzon Street Baroque'. He described how, under the influence of the Sitwells, Italy, Spain and southern Germany provided the model and rooms were filled with

> innumerable pieces of hand-painted furniture from Venice and a surprisingly abundant supply of suspicious Canalettos. At the same time a markedly ecclesiastical note is struck by the forests of twisted Baroque candlesticks . . . old leather-bound hymn books cunningly hollowed out to receive cigarettes, and exuberant gilt prie-dieux ingeniously transformed into receptacles for gramophone records. And all the little Fabergé knick-knacks and Dresden china shepherdesses are finally routed by a noble army of martyrs from the Salzkammergut whose plaster writhings are rendered properly decorative by a liberal application of iridescent paint.

This house must be an almost unique survival of this ephemeral style.

The interior has a curious scent, reminiscent of pot-pourri. The furniture is mostly card, with the details in barbola paste, a popular modelling material of the time.

Now painted as stucco, the exterior was originally small brickwork and the details have been embellished by Mrs Haskell.

FARNHAM HOUSE

LATE EIGHTEENTH CENTURY

Height   *48in*   *(122cm)*
Width   *35in*   *(89cm)*
Depth   *17 ½in*   *(44cm)*   *excluding steps*

THIS DELIGHTFUL LATE EIGHTEENTH-CENTURY HOUSE was acquired many years ago in an open-air market for the now inconceivable sum of £25. It has an unusual arrangement of doors on the landing. Alcoves in the dining room and a chairback rail were (regrettably) added by myself. It is mostly furnished with present-day toy furniture.

This is a tall, professionally made house, with large-scale stucco markings on the sides, and heavy quoining and small brickwork on the front façade. It has thin glazing bars and the heavy front door at the top of the steps is painted green. It formerly had a lock, as did most early houses.

The front opens in one wing, which inside preserves remains of some pretty diaper-patterned paper (left). There are six rooms, a hall, staircase and two landings. The landings, which are at the rear, both have white doors leading to small rooms at the front of the house. A late Victorian doll in a blue dress guards one door. The hall has a tall 1930s red-lacquer clock.

The study. This room has some excellent furniture: a Biedermeier Waltershausen secretaire with green lining paper, an Evans and Cartwright fireplace, and an unusual early nineteenth-century English cabinet, with drawers and glazed shelves with imitation books above, in thin mahogany ornamented with black mouldings. The wallpaper is modern.

The kitchen. On the modern dresser is a set of Saxon turned wooden plates lined in blue. The German stove is in red-enamelled tinplate.

The drawing room. This bright room, with modern gold-starred wallpaper and a woolwork carpet, has a small Evans and Cartwright fireplace. There are Waltershausen pieces, including a square piano, a sewing table and a chaise-longue. A gilt brass jardinière contains potted plants. The two small Grödnertal dolls date from about 1830.

MARBLE HALL

circa 1800

Height 31¹/₂in (80cm)
Width 42in (107cm)
Depth 17in (43cm)

T HIS HOUSE IS one of the few in the collection which have their original contents, in this case mostly of the same date as the house or earlier. I have added the doll (a 1950s wax angel!), the teak table and chairs (date unknown), and the cradle and looking glass (*circa* 1800).

A Pembroke table (above) with two long flaps has a red painted top with a design of trailing flowers, with a white border dotted in green; underneath is an ink inscription which seems to read 'Mrs Huddle Wood gave'. The flower decoration on this table is identical to that on the wall clock in the Mahogany House (see pages 27–9), thus identifying this class of furniture with a London maker. A painted side table (below) of the same period has a print of a lady and gentleman standing in front of their house, perhaps cut out from an early children's book.

This is a simple cupboard, in plain wood, with painted windows. It does, however, have a fine cutout balustrade, and two doors in the façade, each with four panels. The one on the left would open into the hall and the one on the right is the servants' entrance. There are also windows painted on the sides of the house and counterpart windows are painted on the interior walls, a thoughtful touch. The house opens in two wings, with a lock.

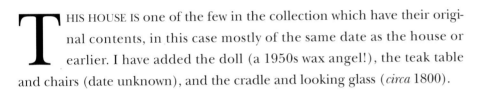

69

There are four rooms only, but the proportions are good.

The parlour. The walls are painted green and the floor has a woolwork rug. The fireplace, with its semicircular Forest grate, is a cast-iron chimney ornament, and there is a fine brass fender. In front stand a pair of elaborate brass firescreens, probably made as ornaments rather than toys, framing beadwork embroidery. There is a large brass-framed picture over the fireplace. The chairs and table are carved in solid teak, and the tilt-top table, also a chimney ornament, is brass. A hanging mahogany corner cupboard has mirror doors and shaped shelves above. This is an eighteenth-century commercial dolls'-house piece, and although all eighteenth-century furniture is scarce, these corner cupboards are comparatively common. A German pewter birdcage is a later addition.

The dining room. The wallpaper is old heavy marbled paper, probably made for book endpapers, and the floor is bare except for a small rug. The furniture is of the very rare type made in England for baby houses in the late eighteenth to early nineteenth centuries, commercially made but somewhat primitive, often with charming naïve decorations. Here are four wooden side chairs painted green, splashed with flowers in red and white. There is also a solid wood long-case clock with a real watch face attached; this was once a watch holder.

The kitchen. This has plain, unpainted walls and floor. The chimneybreast, like the one in the parlour, is made separately from the house and is supported on a block of wood at its rear, a most unusual feature. In the fireplace is an early free-standing brass grate with an iron back. Above is the original brass clockwork jack, and a rack for the spits. The lower part of the turning mechanism has become detached and is lying on the table. On the wall is a built-in set of shelves, the supports with decorative shaping. There is a very full complement of original tin kitchen utensils, including bellows, enamelled in orange; ash pan; small oven or plate warmer; kettle on stand; fish kettle; double saucepan; meat screen with jack; sieve; large sieve for ashes; pail with pouring lip; candlestick and dariole mould.

The bedroom. This has early wallpaper with an all-over pattern of small brown flower sprigs. The floor has a small rug. The large mid-eighteenth-century four-poster bed (just visible in it is a wax doll) has early flowered chintz hangings, bound and tied back with a narrow green-striped linen tape. The curtains to the painted windows are matching. The mahogany toy chest of drawers is of the type made by John Bubb of Long Lane, Bermondsey, London, in the early nineteenth century, but is unmarked. The swing dressing mirror, which is a fine-quality miniature piece of about 1800, and the rocking cradle have been added.

The house is covered almost entirely with a thick, rough, grey plaster finish, scored to imitate stone. For some unexplained reason, this coat is missing from the right side of the house; possibly that side once stood against a wall, but this would have blocked one of the windows and impeded the opening of the front. There are windows, either quatrefoil or pointed with two or three lights, on all three floors, and two long windows on the left side and one on the right. The plaster decorations on the front include cherubs heads and a dancing cherub over the front door. The front door is oak, but does not open. The two lancet windows on either side of the portico light two small 'guardrooms', which are inaccessible from inside or out; these windows also occur at Waynflete Tower. The matching base on which the house stands is a box open at the back. The front of the house opens in one piece, including the columns which support the two towers. These are mounted on castors, an ingenious method to support the heavy weight of the two towers.

REGENCY GOTHICK

EARLY NINETEENTH CENTURY

Height	*53in*	*(135cm)*	*excluding base*
Width	*43in*	*(109cm)*	
Depth	*26in*	*(66cm)*	*including turrets*
Base	*24in*	*(61cm)*	*high*

View through window above portico.

T HIS IS A TRULY 'GOTHICK' CASTLE, the 'k' signifying that the style is the frivolous eighteenth-century variety, not the serious mid-Victorian conception of a truly Christian architecture. In fact, the design harks back to the earliest revival of Gothic architecture, as it has a nearly identical counterpart in Waynflete Tower (*shown above left*), once a gatehouse of the palace of the fifteenth-century bishops of Winchester at Esher. In the early eighteenth century the architect William Kent was commissioned to design a house for Henry Pelham on this site; he retained the gatehouse, adding the quatrefoil windows and the porch, which are charming features of both the tower and the dolls' house. Later, when the Gothick revival had become high fashion, Horace Walpole was much struck by Waynflete Tower, remarking, 'Kent was Kentissime there'. Quite why the dolls' house is so similar to the tower is a mystery. In any event, dolls' houses in the Gothick style are particularly fetching and fairly rare.

In the Regency period Gothick was still a light-hearted style, suitable for seaside villas and follies, so its use for a dolls' house is understandable, but it would still be interesting to know the origins of this elaborate building. Unfortunately, nothing was known about previous owners when it was acquired at auction, empty of all furniture except the fireplaces, the kitchen dresser, the roller towel in the scullery and the rather utilitarian cream-linen roller blinds.

There are seven rooms, but no staircase. When the house is opened, parts of each room are separated, as they are within the towers. Five of the rooms have early, if not original, wallpapers.

Bedroom 1. This room has a charming paper in blue and gold, showing Chinese figures in a garden setting. It is on a small scale, so was probably either designed as a lining – perhaps for a tea poy, or for a fan. The carpet is a piece of paisley. The sleigh bed is mahogany, as are the bed steps; beside the bed is a small folding card table with a pink velvet top. All these are probably English made. There is also a Waltershausen marble-topped dressing table. Nearby is what appears to be a Waltershausen wardrobe, but this is a very rare bachelor's folding bed which, in a bed-sitting room in Victorian lodgings, could be folded up during the day to save space and embarrassment if a lady entered. The modern doll is in her nightdress.

The saloon. The wall decorations here are unusually formal and elaborate. On the back two full-length mirrors are divided by three panels, each with filigree paper borders, white grounds and coloured fancy panels with early Victorian girls in oval frames. This style of wallpaper decoration was particularly popular about 1840, being especially a French production, known as a 'décor', or in English as 'pilaster-and-panel'. It is possible that this wallpaper was put in some years after the house was made. The ceiling has a paper rose and corner pieces. The side walls are similar to the rear, with the overmantel mirror having a gilt card surround. Underneath is a brass and steel 'model' grate in an alabaster surround. The carpet is a piece of Berlin woolwork in a geometric pattern. Furniture includes an alabaster pedestal table, a stool with a beadwork top, two gilt metal *étagères* and a marble-topped Waltershausen console table. The centre table and the gilt harp are both modern reproductions. At the back of the room is a small Gothic Waltershausen cabinet on a sewing table. The scene shows the entertainment of an elegantly dressed Chinese visitor, with a parrot on his shoulder and a moulded hat, by three dolls in original silk dresses, one about 1830 in brown, one a young girl in pink and the other a lady in a big brown velvet hat and matching paletot, with a beaded skirt, all these being Grödnertals. In addition, there is an early wax in pantelettes and a lace dress, with braided blonde plaits and a tiny blue hat. By the tea table, laid with a modern Royal Worcester china tea-seat, is a boy in velvet coat and britches from the 1860s.

Bedroom 2. This has an attractive early green and gilt diamond-pattern paper, a common type of design in dolls' houses for most of the nineteenth-century. The woolwork carpet has a geometric design. The beds are a white-painted metal one and a pewter Diessen swinging cradle. On the floor is an old fabric-lined straw layette basket. A Waltershausen small chest and toilet table complete the furniture, but there are also two Grödnertal dolls, one with a yellow comb and the other much smaller.

The Nelson room. This library commemorates the great hero; his bust is on a stand to the right and his portraits on the wall at the back. Over the fireplace is a coloured print of the Admiralty boardroom. The walls are covered with an old red-flock wallpaper with a gilt filigree border; the carpet is a piece of paisley fabric. The clock with a Cupid started life as a thimble-case. The furniture is of the high quality that German makers were able to achieve when they worked to a slightly larger than usual scale. The Waltershausen cabinet on a stand has dummy books; there is a fall-front secretaire and a circular table with a complex extending mechanism. To complete the naval scene, I have provided a miniature globe inscribed 'Lane's Pocket Globe, London, 1818', with a modern mahogany stand so that it can revolve, for library use. It was acquired in a case with the constellations shown inside. The seated gentleman is the First Lord of the Admiralty, a Grödnertal of the Regency period, in a short jacket with a high collar and tight silk pantaloons. Before him on the desk is a tiny watch and chain, given to me by Flora Gill Jacobs. He is receiving an American Admiral, also from the Washington Museum, who was made about half a century later than the other.

The scullery. Although quite frequently found in eighteenth-century houses, a scullery is uncommon at this date, perhaps because of a snobbish attitude to the domestic area below stairs. It is well equipped with a brick copper and a shallow sink resting on a brick base. The sink is filled by a tap from a wall tank, which would have been filled by a pump. On the wall is a fixed rail for a linen roller towel, the only accessory remaining when the house was acquired.

The chapel. The altar is placed in the turret half of the room, which is imagined as the chapel of a Catholic family. On the walls behind the altar, which were bare, I have put marbled paper. Otherwise, the paper is the same as that of the adjoining bedroom. There are pewter candlesticks, candelabra, etc., and a bisque priest in a chasuble has a tiny miniature missal.

The kitchen. This has a bare wood floor, blue-painted walls, and an Evans and Cartwright tinplate stove. The dresser and a high shelf are built in. The long-case clock is twentieth century. If there ever was a spit, there are no remains of it. The kitchen equipment, all of course added, includes a sugar loaf, a copper jelly mould and a pewter toast-rack with a rather desiccated piece of toast. There are two common peg wooden dolls, and in a rocking chair before the fire a country woman sits, imagined to be the local butter-and-egg woman taking a rest on her weary round.

DURWARD'S HALL

EARLY NINETEENTH CENTURY

Height	*58in*	*(147cm)*
Width	*43in*	*(109cm)*
Depth	*22¹/₂in*	*(43cm)*

T HIS BABY HOUSE belonged to the Vansey family of Halstead, Essex, and is dated by family tradition to the last days of George III. It was bought by Mr Broadhurst of Durwards Hall, Kelvedon, Essex. When Durwards Hall was sold, the baby house was left in the attic, where I saw it five years later and bought it from the daughter of the new owner. The furniture had been dispersed, but the 'new' furniture dates mostly from the late eighteenth and early nineteenth centuries.

The house has a flat roof and a large, plain façade which hooks on in one piece, is painted in a tea colour and is marked out as stucco. The windows are four-paned (the first-floor glazing bars are missing). The front door is six-panelled, in mahogany.

The interior has three large rooms: a bedroom, a drawing room and a kitchen.

The sofa (below) is well made and unusual, of the English Regency period with lion-head decorations, mahogany with grey and black striped silk upholstery. The seat cushion is made separately, with pink tufting, resting on a base of yellow glazed cotton.

The drawing room. This has a cast-iron fireplace with a Forest grate of the type made as chimney ornaments, decorated with cherubs, nereids and classical females. There is a bordered blue carpet and modern wallpaper. Tables include one in papier mâché, painted with a bird, and an eighteenth-century inlaid side table. A miniature cabinet of fine workmanship with glazed shelves above dates also from the late eighteenth century and contains a collection of glass. There are many accessories, including a tiny cordial glass, a silver tea-set with a kettle on a stand, a turned wood German tea-set, busts in Parian ware of Lord Byron and the Hermes of Praxiteles, and a sand picture of about 1800, painted with coloured sands made to adhere to the picture surface. This is probably from the Isle of Wight, where souvenirs made of Alum Bay sands are traditional. Three very different dolls, one a peg wooden, one a wax doll dressed by me as an elderly lady and one a bisque baby, inhabit this room.

The bedroom. The floor has woolwork rugs and the wallpaper is modern. The furniture is of much interest. The bed is a turned wooden four-poster of the early nineteenth century. The two 'foxy red' Evans and Cartwright dining chairs have the maker's name impressed on the back legs unusually clearly. There is also an elegant dark-green-painted Evans and Cartwright dining chair, with a seat painted white with small sprigs of roses, to imitate embroidery. This decoration was probably added at some period after the chair was purchased. The Evans and Cartwright fireplace is in a white marbled wood surround. There are also two English mahogany washstands and a mahogany-veneer chest of drawers, with handles made from pearl buttons. I have also added some modern Swedish miniature furniture in the Empire style. A tiny sampler worked in black thread is initialled 'MHD', but there is no date. Note also a mahogany bonnet stand and a miniature Bible of 1820.

The kitchen. A blue-painted room which has a built-in dresser and a table attached to the wall, both painted grey. There is also a built-in sink and original plate racks. The tinplate range, with its oven and boiler, is all of a piece with the enamelled surround and mantelshelf. The surround and shelf are yellow, with blue lining. On the mantelshelf are two japanned tin trays, the earlier oval one being black with a painted flower. Equipment includes an early charcoal flat iron, a coffee grinder and a heavy pewter urn for hot water. On the dresser is a service of white china.

84

STACK HOUSE

1820

Height 36in (91cm)
Width 40in (102cm)
Depth 15½in (39cm)

THIS HOUSE WAS MADE at Settle in Yorkshire, but is quite uncharacteristic of any houses in that district, which are of stone. (It is more characteristic of those in Sussex; for example, in Lewes.) It remained at Stack House in Settle with one family for more than 100 years until sold to the late Mr Charles Forte. As I mentioned in talking about his other house, Portobello (see pages 20–3), this Charles Forte was an antiques dealer in Sussex with whom I was friendly. It was then sold to Miss M. Titcombe (also a friend of mine). Most of the wallpaper is original and the furniture came with the house, having been supplied by the previous owners. The child doll, and the hall and dining room wallpaper, I have added. The house is a complete reflection of life in about 1835, with little of a much later date.

The Tunbridge circular pedestal table with inlay was originally intended as a novelty pin-holder.

The façade is of painted wood, very detailed in its depiction of windows with curtains and the front door, and lifts off. The kitchen window shows a typical feature of the time, recommended in Loudon's *Encyclopaedia of Cottage, Farm and Villa Architecture* of 1830, a wire blind to keep out flies when the lower sash is up. Peering over this, in *trompe-l'oeil*, is a maidservant's head, forever watching for visitors to appear.

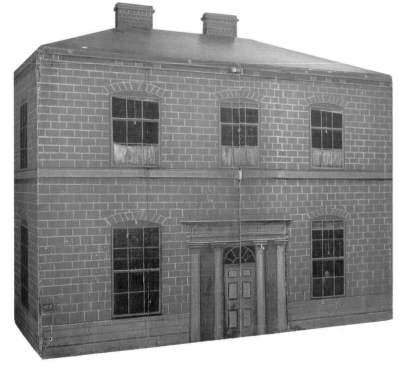

The interior. This is quite simple in design, having four rooms, a staircase hall and landing.

The dining room. This has a paisley carpet and modern wallpaper. The fireplace is Evans and Cartwright. Two Waltershausen rosewood cabinets with bone pillars above supporting shelves are used as sideboards. At the rear of the room is a vitrine filled with a quantity of old miniature striped and fluted glass, and two glass wine bottles stand on the rosewood sideboard. A gilt brass birdcage is on its own stand. By the fireplace is an unusually shaped coal scuttle in tinplate with gilt decoration. Above, on the mantelpiece, is a gilt clock.

The kitchen. This is simply furnished. The walls are plain wood and the floor is marked out with paving bricks. On the wall is a hanging set of shelves, used as a dresser. The table, chair and open cupboard are all strictly utilitarian. A wooden fire-surround has a tin kitchen grate with sloping back and two hobs. The early tin equipment includes a plate warmer, a grater, lidded pans and a colander. There are some pewter pieces, including a set of early dishes impressed with cornucopias, and a long, thin, black board for writing shopping lists on. A doll in a bonnet and print dress presides.

The drawing room. This has a pretty wallpaper with gold stars, and a carpet of check wool embroidery in blue, white and black. The fireplace is Evans and Cartwright tinplate. Waltershausen pieces include a desk with turquoise lining paper, a green-silk-covered Biedermeier-style sofa, two chairs and a rocker. The Waltershausen sewing table has the usual Empire lyre-shaped base and mirrored top. Pictures include three rococo-style gilt brass dolls'-house frames.

Bedroom 2. The wallpaper is striped grey, with an interesting green and pink border in spirals, and the floor is covered with a fabric carpet. This house is well furnished, without the overcrowding common in the latter part of the century. Two early chairs in the foreground have yellow tinplate imitation-rush seats and brown cast-metal frames, with blue and white flowers on the crest rails. These chairs had labels on saying 'old Auley furniture', which led to my using the name in my early books for this type of furniture, as it was the only clue I had to its origin. Recently, much of it has been identified as being made by Evans and Cartwright of Wolverhampton. The remainder of the furniture is Waltershausen rosewood, including a half-tester bed with grey spotted, floral-printed curtains with braid edging and tie backs, a wardrobe with a large oval mirror and a chest of drawers with a toilet mirror. Accessories include a gilt pewter firescreen with pink silk inset and a pewter hanging wall-tidy, lined with cream silk, bordered with, and hung from, pink ruched silk ribbon. The rarest object is a Waltershausen hanging cabinet for keys, on the left-hand wall near the front.

The hall. Here a marbled archway leads to a realistic stairwell. The wallpaper and carpet are the same as in the dining room. A German tin pendulum clock hangs above a pewter umbrella stand. An early doll (1820–30) in original costume, including striped silk dress, grey silk ribbons, stands beside a tinplate German pram of a later date, enamelled blue with a gilt line.

STRAWBERRY HILL GOTHICK

1820–30

Height	*25¹/₂in*	*(65cm)*
Width	*28in*	*(71cm)*
Depth	*14in*	*(36cm)*

A detail of the warming pan and brass grate from the kitchen.

T HIS IS ANOTHER 'Gothick' dolls' house. As noted in discussing 'Regency Gothick' (see pages 72–9), dolls' houses in this style, pre-dating the Victorian revival inspired by Pugin, are rare.

This house is one of the latest to have a lock; it opens in one wing. The roof is shallow-pitched and partly hidden behind the decorative fretted balustrade. On the façade four slender columns rise to end in icing-sugar pinnacles. The front door also has Gothic tracery and there are mouldings over the door and hood-moulds over the windows. The pink paintwork is, of course, both pretty and a reference to Horace Walpole's Gothick villa at Strawberry Hill on the Thames at Twickenham. Horace Walpole, the dilettante and letter-writer, bought his house, then quite ordinary, in 1747. With the help of friends organized into a 'Committee of Taste', he proceeded to turn it into a Gothick castle, using architectural motifs with enthusiasm but out of their original context, and creating a fanciful showpiece in which he lived a long and comfortable bachelor life. It proved an inspiration for many seaside villas and garden buildings, and is still, though altered, in an excellent state of preservation.

At first sight a plain four-room house, this has a hall and landing but no stairs; behind the two doors are two small, dark rooms. All the wallpapers are new. The rooms are on a small scale, about 1:15, and I have furnished them with a mixture of Regency and Victorian pieces.

The red chairs are a type made in the Erzgebirge area from the Empire period onwards.

The parlour. The tinplate fireplace is by Evans and Cartwright. The chairs and window seat are German Waltershausen in a plain Empire style, with faded silk covers. The woolwork rug is worked with 'Victoria Rgina' (*sic*).

The kitchen. This room has some traces of old papers. At either side of the fireplace here and in the next room are shallow alcoves with arched tops. The furniture is very simple, but there are some nice accessories, including a Dutch oven, used to heat food or plates before the fire, a grater and a warming pan.

The study. This has a small cherrywood secretaire, Waltershausen chairs and a large glazed cabinet. In the fireplace is an English late eighteenth-century brass grate with a tinplate back which is engraved on each side with a wavy pattern, a rare piece.

The house is back-opening and has two single-storey annexes, a dairy and a stable. There is a shallow-pitched roof behind a parapet, and the façade is scored with brickwork.

CHERRY HALL, DUBLIN

1825

Height of main house	*24in*	*(61cm)*	
Width	*49¹/₂in*	*(126cm)*	*including the wide base*
Depth of main house	*12¹/₂in*	*(32cm)*	

THIS WAS AN INHERITED HOUSE, in an Anglo-Irish family for three generations, who lived in Merrion Square, Dublin. None of the accessories, nor any furniture, came with the dolls' house, which was quite derelict. The staircase was missing and paint poured over the roof. Note the groom in his livery and the carriage horse. The hens, goats, and pigs seemed to be suitable for this Irish farm house.

The stable is crudely made, but has a fine yellow cart with a black lining, two horses and a bisque coachman, complete with black topper and caped red coat. The dairy, which is on the other side of the house, has a wooden churn and shallow bowls for separating cream.

CHERRY HALL, DUBLIN

The kitchen. This has a mixture of old and modern pieces. The old include a wool mat with a cat worked on it, two painted, turned wooden plates with red flowers on green leaves and a soft metal cutlery box with pewter cutlery.

The study. At the back is an old German circular table; the rest of the furniture is modern miniature. The chandelier is old gilt brass.

THE PEDIMENT HOUSE

1827

Height	*56in*	*(142cm)*	*excluding stand*
Width	*37in*	*(94cm)*	
Depth	*15¹/₂in*	*(39cm)*	

The parlour. This has the original grey and white floral wallpaper and a mat of Berlin woolwork. The sand picture of a castle is made of natural coloured sands, chiefly from Alum Bay on the Isle of Wight. The mahogany square piano, at which a peg wooden doll is seated, is English, early nineteenth century. The doors are painted in white distemper, and the curtains are in an old printed chintz. The dark wood, later nineteenth-century German drawing-room suite of sofa and chairs is covered in pink velvet.

THE PEDIMENT HOUSE

The façade of this house, which is not shown, is very plain. The pediment has a large circular window with the date 1827 written above. There was also a lock and key. Note the old wallpapers of beautiful colour and pattern, revealed when modern paper has been peeled off. There are only four rooms, and no stairs. The attic behind the pediment would have been used to store furniture.

On the drawing room table is an ivory cup-and-ball set, a favourite indoor game, giving exercise in bad weather. It will be remembered that Jane Austen was admired by her nieces for her skill at this game.

The kitchen. The early enamelled tinplate fireplace is formed from a toy kitchen with its side wings folded back. The pots on the shelf are soldered on. This type of toy kitchen is early nineteenth-century English, with its hob grate and unusual tin wheel for turning meat on a spit. The fireplace is set into a hole cut in the back wall of the dolls' house and contains a grid under the grate, to provide an underfloor draught for the fire.

The drawing room. This room has two large, four-paned windows at the back, behind which I have arranged some scenery. The striking wallpaper, with columns of arsenical green foliage with blue flowers, dominates the room, and indicates how a bold disregard of scale can give triumphant results. The fireplace is painted paper, with gilt and silver trims. The furniture includes an inlaid Italian table and some miniatures made originally for the Japanese Doll Festival. The two early nineteenth-century firescreens in mahogany with pink velveteen are English, commercially made about 1830. The Waltershausen ebonized table with gilt transfers has an unusual gate-leg arrangement with the top folding diagonally in two triangles. The tea-set on the Japanese table is turned wood. The tall doll in a silk dress is papier-mâché, and the little girl is an early Grödnertal.

THE
REGENCY HOUSE

circa 1835

Height	*48in*	*(122cm)*
Width	*44¹/₂in*	*(113cm)*
Depth	*18in*	*(46cm)*

T HIS HOUSE CAME from Ireland. It has a fine façade, but poor workman-ship inside. Originally it had two doors at the back. The wallpapers are all new, the decoration and contents all added, excepting the beautiful set of early 'rout' chairs, including seats for two dancers and the chaperon.

This is a back-opening house, the shallow-pitched roof surrounded with a widow's walk, the balustrade rather similar to that on houses in Maine, USA. The paintwork is grey-green, with large brickwork in dark red. The façade is late Georgian in style, with two Venetian windows and a semicircular fanlight over the front door, but the windows have four Victorian-style panes. The slender pillars on each side of the door and of the façade are attractive.

The parlour. This is decorated with a striped paper, but preserves the remains of an attractive old paper with stripes of flowers on a green-dotted, white ground. The suite of salon furniture is German, in a Regency style but probably dating from the early twentieth century.

The five rooms are on a large scale, about
1:10, and there are no stairs. There is a large
hall, in which the cook is hobnobbing with a
drunken fellow wearing an apron and
holding a bottle and a beer mug.

The library. I installed the library, making
all the bookcases and books. The jib door to
the drawing room is lined with the spines of
books, a frequent decorative trick in English
country-house libraries. Sometimes the
books have jokey titles, such as The Snakes
of Ireland (there are no snakes in Ireland:
they were driven out by St Patrick). The
pedestal table is German, the figure a
modern one. On the table is an old glass
ink-bottle with a metal top. The chairs are
modern brass, probably Indian.

The drawing room. This has modern French wallpaper, copied from the well-known Jouy toile *Le Ballon de Gonesse*, 1784. The design has been reversed from the original cotton print. The room contains some rare furniture. To the left is a Waltershausen Biedermeier-style chest with a grey marble top. On each side are miniature Spode willow-pattern jars. The cherrywood sewing table has a Continental porcelain figure of Napoleon. A gilt brass standing birdcage contains a coloured-glass parrot. On the rear wall an upright black Waltershausen pianoforte of about 1850 is transfer-decorated in the Gothic revival manner. Very rare are the three red-painted wooden mock-bamboo Regency rout chairs with wire stretchers, English commercial pieces of the period. Their seats are carved to imitate rush, similar to Evans and Cartweight metal chairs of the same period and style. The circular card table with a folding top is a well-made English piece, probably from later in the nineteenth century. A mid-Victorian china doll stands in front of a Waltershausen sofa of the same date. Beside her posture the pale figures of Canova's *Three Graces* in Parian ware, the original being recently the subject of much transatlantic argument. The lamp table and the carpet are modern.

THE TOLL HOUSE

EARLY NINETEENTH CENTURY

Height	*18¹/₂in*	*(47cm)*
Width	*17¹/₂in*	*(44cm)*
Depth	*10in*	*(25cm)*

THIS SMALL MODEL of a toll house is painted with large bricks. It opens at the back and had no original contents. The idea for the decoration of the house dates from a stay in 1972 at West Dean House in Sussex, the former home of the James family. The West Dean Foundation had allowed me to make an inventory of their magnificent Nuremberg dolls' house. By chance, on my last evening, Mr Edward James flew in unexpectedly from Mexico and sat at the same table. I have never, I think, been so impressed and fascinated by any personality as I was by his. When he announced that he would meet me again the following evening, I had sadly to say that I needed to return home for my brother's birthday. In any case, Mr James always acted on impulse and might quite as easily have decided to fly to Mexico or on to Paris.

This explains why, when I read of the dispersal on 7 June 1986 of the contents of Monkton House, Mr James's hideaway in the grounds of West Dean, I determined to make a 'remembrance'. The Toll House, which had been waiting for attention for some year, is castellated, and is part of West Dean, and has similar Gothic windows. To the windows I now added blue, red and green glass, and I lined the upper-room walls and ceiling with mirror. Mr James slept at Monkton in a bed modelled on Napoleon's funeral car; a modern bed was gilded, the narrow ends of garden bamboo poles were cut and gilded, and two corners from an Italian papier mâché tray were sawn off and glued to head and foot. Palm leaves were cut from stiff green cotton and partly gilded. A supermarket cardboard food tray was covered in an old gilt leather belt, edged with gold lace-paper, and hung with draperies in dark-blue chiffon velvet edged with yellow braid. The tray, of course, was the canopy, so was glued to the ceiling. A 2-in (5-cm) early Staffordshire figure of Napoleon stands on a marbled wedding-cake pillar nearby. An 1880 chair was gilded and the upholstery painted blue, a chandelier and a Baroque mirror added.

Downstairs the room follows one in Monkton in being lined with ivy paper (fortunately, so was a bathroom of mine) and a leopard-print carpet to imitate the wolfhounds' paw-prints woven for Mr James, with matching curtains, was added. I made on a cardboard base the famous sofa in red satin 'in the shape of Mae West's lips' and a mad chair without a back (a round seat, a goose's wishbone, and two little metal hands formerly cuff-links). A marbled triangular table, potted palms and framed pictures commissioned by Edward James from René Magritte (taken from the Tate Gallery catalogue, reduced by Xerox) completed the lower room when a macaw, a species fondly regarded by its owner, was added – but of course flying free. A carved bear bought long ago in Switzerland was painted to ressemble the stuffed polar-bear lamp, which was the gift of Salvador Dali to Mr James, and now holds a lamp. This was the final and satisfactory conclusion of the furnishing, for it had been rather a matter of pride that nothing had been bought especially for this little *jeu d'esprit*. Its history, and the paragraph on Monkton House taken from the National Trust report, I pasted on the back, under the heading 'In Memory of Edward James'.

WHITEWAY

1850

Height	*43¹/₂in*	*(110cm)*
Width	*57¹/₂in*	*(145cm)*
Depth	*18in*	*(46cm)*

THIS FORMERLY STOOD in Saltram House in Devon. The late Lord Morley (d. 1962) gave it to his footman for his little daughter. When the National Trust took over Saltram House, the dolls' house had by then been sold to a local antiques dealer, who offered it to the Trust so that it could be returned to Saltram. As it was not a replica of Saltram House but related to an earlier house, Whiteway near Chudleigh, Devon, the Trust was not interested in acquiring it. Most of the furniture belonged to the house, notably the books, beds, needlework carpets and the maps in the schoolroom.

The curator of Saltram, Patrick Dawes, recounted to me in a letter:

> a lady's maid of the third Countess of Morley (d. 1910) said that the dolls' house was considered an item of outstanding merit by all the members of the staff of Saltram. She went on to describe how the dolls'-house children were in bed, and there were little miniature hip baths and chamber pots, and a footman in livery in one of the reception rooms and the servants bustling about.

Whiteway was in the ownership of the Morley family until about 1920. It was originally built by Montague Edward Parker, the younger brother of John, 1st Lord Boringdon, whose parents built Saltram in 1750. Montague Parker's granddaughter, Harriet Sophia, married her second cousin, Edward, 2nd Earl of Morley, and as both her brothers died unmarried she inherited Whiteway after her parents' death, and the two properties were reunited. Mr Dawes suggested that this dolls' house was made for her daughter, Lady Emily Catherine Parker, born in 1846, who never married and lived with her mother at Whiteway all her life. However, there is no actual proof of this, or indeed that the dolls' house was ever at Whiteway.

The real Whiteway is a red-brick, three-storey mansion which has a pediment with a bust within an oval and a central porch with four Tuscan columns. The garden front, according to Pevsner, has a canted full-height bay, and Venetian windows to the left and right. The dolls' house is not therefore a copy, although there are a few similarities.

The drawing-room clock, china and metal with a classical figure, probably should have a dome.

A German pewter filigree perambulator, from the hall, of the kind made by the Schweizer factory in Diessen, which was established in the eighteenth century and still flourishes.

Bedroom 2. This has pale pink wallpaper and a woolwork carpet with a design of small roses on a wine-coloured ground. The original French bed is hung from mahogany rods with a scarlet sprig pattern to match the curtains. The corner fireplace has a cast-iron Forest grate with the head of the young Queen Victoria in relief, like that on the early pennies, a type of grate which has been found in other houses of this period. I have added the late nineteenth-century German lithographed bedroom suite, of a chest, table, chair, cabinet and dressing table. The chest shows the delightful printed paper floral decorations, the clock surmounted with a picture of a pet dog. A nurse is bending over a baby in the cot.

Bedroom 1. The walls are pale blue and the striped woolwork carpet is original, as is the furniture, except for the dressing-table stool. The fireplace matches the one in the other bedroom (see above). There is an English mahogany bed, washstand and dressing table of the same general kind found in Mrs Bryant's dolls' house at the Museum of Childhood, Bethnal Green, London. The four-poster has original yellow silk hangings, and there is a contemporary miniature chest of drawers with white china knobs. Also in this room is a small oil painting of Whiteway house in Devon, to replace an earlier lost photograph.

The drawing room. The blue silk wall-covering is edged with gilt metal fillets, and the carpet is a bold woolwork pattern. The fireplaces, here and in the other principal rooms, are very realistically made, so that in order to provide sufficient depth for them, holes have been cut in the back of the house, to which shallow boxes have been attached. The furniture is mainly metal, including an Evans and Cartwright pedestal table with added gilding, a gilt brass table and whatnot, and three sets of mirror-backed hanging shelves.

The house opens in two wings, one being hinged, showing three floors, with a hall, staircase, two landings and six main rooms. The top landing has been divided to provide an extra room, now used for trunks. Like the real Whiteway, it has good neoclassical 'marble' fireplaces. It was built at a period when ladies were not expected to have much interest in domestic affairs, apart from ordering meals, and there is no kitchen. There is, however, a feeling of great comfort and good order in the house. All the wallpapers are original except for the hall, stairs and the trunk room.

The dining room. The walls are covered with a red quilted silk material, with a gilt fillet, and the carpet is red plush. The dining suite is a German unvarnished wood, and the heavy sideboard and grandfather clock English. The table is laid with onion-pattern china, an imitation of a Meissen pattern made in vast quantities in Germany for dolls'

houses. A ham, a cold chicken and a plum pudding sit on the sideboard. Many dolls are seated round the table, including a bisque clergyman, a soldier in regimentals and a blonde lady with ringlets. Behind the table is a footman in a red livery (shown on following page). The mahogany butler's tray has several bottles, including labelled liqueurs.

The footman from the dining room (see pages 108–9).

The library. This room is the most unusual in the house, as it is very rare for a Victorian house to have such elaborate built-in fitments as we see here. The wooden bookcases with their false books, also wood, are beautifully made. The wallpaper is similar to that in the nursery, but in green, and the carpet is a complex pattern in bright woolwork. An oil lamp hangs from the ceiling and another, of the type known as a student lamp, is on the table. Beside it is a perpetual calendar dated 3 May. There are two notes on this table which read:

Mrs Montclair
Mme. Leza Fletcher presents her compts. to the families resident at Langdon House. Her manyfold occupations will prevent her from accepting the invitation kindly sent by Mrs Montclair. She hopes the 'housewarming' may be a success and without flames.

Weds. 18 Jany.   18 Whitn. Coll.

and:

Mrs Montclair: Miss Lewis presents her compts. to Mrs Montclair, and has great pleasure in accepting her aimiable invitation for Sat. 21st.

The College, Tuesday.

'The College' is a mystery. Perhaps it was a school; Whittington College in Highgate, London, is an almshouse, so hardly suitable. There are many more accessories, including Bryce's Complete Bible in miniature, a bone ink-stand made to resemble deer's horn, a gilt blotter and a pewter newspaper rack.

The hall. The generously proportioned stairs are constructed round a well.

The day nursery/ schoolroom. The paper has a small gold design on white and the carpet is red plush. The circular Waltershausen table has a complex extending mechanism. The room is full of children, including an early china girl in original short dress with green sash, two bisque girls, two china boys, one with pink lustre shoes, and a little girl with an Alice band. On the walls are mounted maps, contemporary with the house, showing America, the state of Massachusetts and the world. I have added the toys. They are a mixture of old and new, from a little lead horse and an Erzgebirge wooden doll with a feather in her hat to one of Joan Gibson's little toy theatres. The glass case on the right-hand wall, however, is an early piece, containing ten hand-cut paper butterflies, quivering gently.

BELGRAVIA

1850

Height	*44in*	*(112cm)*
Width	*34in*	*(86cm)*
Depth	*18¹/₂in*	*(47cm)*

T HIS WAS THE FIRST HOUSE acquired, during the Second World War in 1944, and in my first book it was called 'Exhibition Year'. It had no furniture, was filthy dirty inside and had five coats of different-coloured paints, which I removed with the aid of shards from broken bottles. The bottom coat was cream, which the house now is. At that time there was no interest in rescuing old houses and the modern aids, scalpels and paint removers, were not thought of. All the furnishings which I have added date from around 1850–60, except for some home-made dolls, the tea-service in silver in the drawing room and two home-made pictures, *No Cross No Crown* and a seaweed picture. The wallpapers are mainly those sold before the war by *Hobbies* or *Handicrafts* magazines for decorating children's dolls' houses.

This is a commercial dolls' house, basically a box-back of the kind made in the London area for about 150 years, but with the attraction of an Italianate façade, with free-standing pillars on the first floor, topped with urns, and more pillars on the second floor. The semicircular tops to the upper-floor windows were popular at this period and similar houses can be found in many Victorian parts of central London. It opens in two wings.

The drawing room. This has a charming starred wallpaper and a Berlin woolwork rug. The walls are crowded with gilt-framed pictures, some in the frames originally used for daguerreotypes. An elderly lady in black is playing the piano; she has a music-stand with original music in manuscript. Note also the Waltershausen work-table with its mirrored lid; it has its original fittings (top). The family album on the piano has real photographs of Queen Victoria and Prince Albert. Two bisque ladies are listening to the music, one sitting on a Waltershausen sofa. The Waltershausen sofa (above), in imitation rosewood, is upholstered in a printed cotton carefully designed to fit its shape – evidence of the sophistication of the German manufacturer.

This is a six-room house, with a
staircase, hall and two landings.
The dog-leg stairs are steep and
narrow, by comparison with earlier
houses. At their foot is an antler
hallstand. On the top landing is a
false window in gilt paper.

The bedroom. Like the drawing
room, this room is furnished with
Waltershausen rosewood,
including a fine half-tester bed,
wardrobe, dressing table and
washstand with a marble top. The
toilet set is in green and pink
striped turned wood and includes
a 'coral' ring stand, at the left on
the dressing table. In the bed lies a
sick lady; she was bought dressed
in her original flannel nightdress,
so she must always have been an
invalid. Her son, in a brown velvet
suit, reads to her from a miniature
Bible. The book is lying on an
English Regency rosewood table,
which was made as a pincushion.

The day nursery. This room, as it would have been in real life, is furnished with an assortment of odd chairs, together with a practical fireguard and towel rail. On the mantelpiece is a tiny Swiss chalet. The treadle sewing machine is in metal. A china nursemaid holds a small girl and bisque twin girls are dressed in red cotton trimmed with ricrac braid.

The night nursery. Here we have two beds and a cradle sheltering the newest arrival, watched over by an old nanny. Note the blue china toilet set and the German pewter workbasket with a fabric bag.

The dining room. Here, amid a clutter of china on the linen tablecloth, grandfather Bosanquet reads the morning paper. Red wallpaper was the traditional choice for dining rooms in the nineteenth century. The furniture is Waltershausen, including a sideboard, chairs, a cabinet with bone turned pillars and the clock on the mantelpiece, also with bone pillars. There is a gilt brass magazine rack on the right.

The kitchen. The floor is covered with American cloth and a rag rug. At the rear is a dresser on which are turned wooden plates from Saxony with a flower decoration; a 1930s red wooden tray has crept in. The housekeeper, with her keys on a chatelaine, is entertaining an early policeman doll, a Victorian 'Peeler', so called after Sir Robert Peel, who founded the police force in the 1840s. This is the only early policeman doll I have ever come across. Between them sits a velveteen tabby cat with bead eyes. There is also a working mousetrap. On the table is a vast plum pudding, as big as the talkative one in *Alice Through the Looking Glass*, and a sirloin of beef dating from 1850. The huge wire dish-cover, to keep off flies, hangs on the wall, indicating the size of the family joints.

WATERLOO VILLAS

MID-NINETEENTH CENTURY

Height	*32 ¹/₂in*	*(83cm)*
Width	*34in*	*(86cm)*
Depth	*17in*	*(43cm)*

THIS IS THAT UNUSUAL FORM of dolls' house: semi-detached, with two front doors and two rooms in each dwelling. The phrase 'semi-detached' sounds so modern, but was used by Emily Eden in the title of her witty novel *The Semi Detached House* in the early nineteenth century. Since it stands in my own house, I have felt freer to use some of the beguiling objects made by craftsmen of the present day. One such was commissioned to make a harp, apologizing that he really could not fit in the true number of strings, and from another came a basket of mushrooms.

With a flat roof, this has a machicolated balustrade around the top and even the chimneys are castle-like. The outside is oil-painted in a stone colour, picked out in dark red, and with the name, Waterloo Villas, in large letters on the front, which opens in two wings. The front doors do not open. There are four rooms only, and no staircase, but each room retains interesting old wallpapers. The house is crowded with a mixture of objects old and new, some of which could not properly fit into a purely period setting. Only a few can be mentioned here. As these are rooms for display, none is furnished as a kitchen or a bedroom.

117

WATERLOO VILLAS

Top left: Mrs Nightingale's parlour/sewing room. The wallpaper here is in the 'pilaster-and-panel' style, also found in Regency Gothick (see pages 72–9). In front of an old filigree fireplace a number of cats are sitting on a half-cross-stitch mat. On the Waltershausen rosewood marble-topped cabinet is a tape measure in the form of a toll-house in turned wood. This is an early piece of Tunbridge ware, quite unlike the mosaic work usually associated with this name.

Top right: Mr Charles's study. Here the wallpaper is a diaper pattern in grey. The dominant eight-bay Gothic-style bookcase was made to order. The circular pedestal table is English and the old brass pendulum clock on the wall is German.

Lower left: Mrs Nightingale's music room. This has an interesting wall treatment of large panels of pink and brown diaper paper with gilt borders. There are two unusual pianos. The one on the right is an English upright toy piano of about 1830, made of a solid block, with gilt paper decorations. The large piano at the back is another early upright toy of about 1820, in this case a Broadwood type with inlay decoration and a green silk panel behind glass. In this room and the next are scattered a set of five unusual Waltershausen chairs.

Lower right: Mr Charles's taxidermy room. Filled with trophies of all kinds, this has a diaper-pattern paper of leaves on a brown ground. Here we see, as examples of his craft, stuffed fish, stuffed birds, mounted butterflies, even an unfortunate unicorn's head, enough to make an environmentalist blanch (a toy farm-horse with a sea shell stuck to its head). The beautiful case of stuffed birds is a fine example of modern craftsmanship. The umbrella in the stand was given to the curate on his resignation by his affectionate congregation.

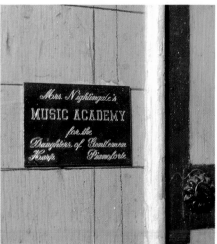

On each front door is hung the brass plate of the occupier, as follows:

Mr Francis Charles,	Mrs Nightingale
Bird-Stuffer to the	MUSIC ACADEMY
NOBILITY	for the
and Gentry	Daughters of Gentlemen
	Harp Pianoforte

Mr Charles I thought of as a curate who had lost his faith and now earned his living as a taxidermist, stuffing the birds and fish which commemorated the prowess of his county neighbours. Mrs Nightingale is his widowed sister. Cats abound in this house, for both are, or would otherwise be, lonely people. The house opens in two wings. A brass birdcage hangs in one window.

COBURG

NINETEENTH CENTURY

Height   *78in*   *(198cm)*   *including stand*
Width   *97½in*   *(248cm)*   *including wings*
Depth   *24in*   *(50cm)*

COBURG WAS ALMOST in the category of 'the ones that got away', about which a whole memoir could be written. A few weeks had been spent visiting privately owned houses in East Anglia for an exhibition. The always difficult cross-country journey by public transport, via London and returning to Oxford the same day, had been made frequently, and eventually came the opening day of the exhibition. Then one of the members of the Dolls' House Society said that the auction of a large dolls' house would be held on the following day. The heart quailed at the thought of another day's round trip, but then that was against the sight of the enormous, smoke-blackened structure, its staircase in fifty pieces in a shoebox, and the splendid casement windows, some missing. What was to be done? There had been a fire in Harrods' Furniture Depository and the house, which had owed its rent, could now legally be sold to pay for its keep. Very professionally, the depository was unwilling, or perhaps was simply unable, to give its history or any details of earlier ownership.

The amazing house is striking not only for its size but also for its chinoiserie architecture. This style, popular on the Continent and in Britain in the eighteenth and early nineteenth centuries, was generally used for pavilions and garden buildings. It was considered to be fanciful and amusing rather than seriously architectural, on a par with 'Gothick' and 'Hindou'. Here it is used for a substantial mansion with two service wings, one for the kitchen and the other for stables. No other dolls' houses in this style are known and no real house with a near resemblance has been seen. It seems extraordinary that so large an object should have no recorded history, but since the house was acquired in 1980, enquiries have failed even to establish finally a country of origin. The only clues are 'Coburg 318' chalked on the roof, possibly implying an Anglo-German origin, and the still unidentified coat of arms on the

The armorial shield, probably belonging to the house's original owners, has not so far been identified, despite expert investigation. It seems to show wolves' heads and birds, and may belong to a Suffolk family.

The house is marked out with stonework and painted a soft yellow-ochre to represent stone or stucco. The amazing roofline of the main house is echoed in the two service wings. The casement windows, with their distinctive outlines, open outwards, unlike Continental windows which often open inwards. The cupboards beneath were no doubt used for storing toys. The front door has narrow glass windows on either side.

front. Some features, such as the built-in metal fireplaces and the outward-opening casements, suggest an English origin, but the date of manufacture, although certainly nineteenth century, is uncertain.

The house was acquired without any furniture, apart from a gilt metal chandelier, a mahogany-framed mirror and some German lithographed pictures in gilt-embossed metal frames. On the back of one picture was the price, 3d., and on another a label, 'Charles Morrell, 168–170 Oxford Street', a well-known London toyshop. I eventually decided to furnish the house, in an allusion to the name 'Coburg', as the hunting box of one of Queen Victoria's more obscure relatives, such as Hesse-Cassel, or Hohenzollern-Sigmarigen, or even Hohenlohe-Langeburg, the supposed time being 1872–80. Unfortunately, in only one room was the original wallpaper preserved. Unusually, therefore, to create the intended impression, modern miniature furnishings and papers were extensively used in this house.

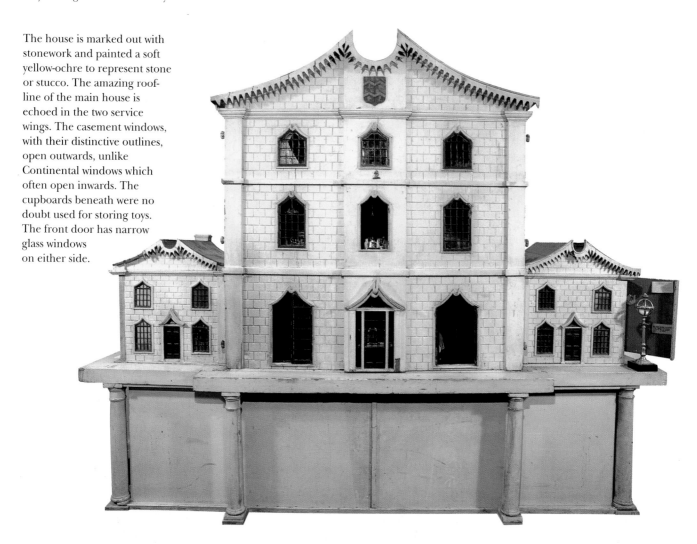

The drawing room. The walls are covered in old fabric and the furniture includes decorative gilt pieces in the style of the period. A bisque lady in an 1870s dress stands on the left and behind her, on the rear wall, is a portrait of Queen Victoria in old age.

The stable wing. There is a tack room at the rear, and four stalls, containing modern 'Julip' horses, two carriage horses, one hunter and one cob. The stalls have been named Albany, Teck, Balmoral and Sefton, the last to commemorate a horse badly injured in a terrorist bomb attack in Hyde Park in 1982.

Bedroom 1. Furnishings include an old mock-bamboo '*étagerè*' in gilt metal and a bead-embroidered wall pocket for a watch. This room has mock bamboo chairs and a green 'lacquer' chest of drawers.

The chapel. This indicates a Roman Catholic family in residence; it has three rows of pews and gilt candlesticks. The ceiling I have decorated with stars to show the constellations as they were at the time and date of the acquisition of Coburg!

122

The music room. This is papered with the gilt Chinese paper once used for lining tea-chests. The furniture includes a Waltershausen upright piano and an antique gilt chandelier.

Bedroom 2. This has attractive original purple and turquoise foliage wallpaper. On the elegantly draped dressing table is an Erzgebirge turned wooden ring stand, with a branch of 'coral' to hold the rings. On the other side is a typical Waltershausen sewing table with a lyre-shaped base, open to show the sewing compartments. On the wall hang several portraits, including one of the Princess of Prussia.

The dining hall. This room stretches the width of the main house, with an unusual double staircase meeting and redividing to reach the first floor. It is panelled in wood and has a painted ochre floor. An early Victorian tinplate fireplace has a brass surround. Hunting trophies, including a rather unlikely elephant, deck the walls, and a bisque gentleman in hunting pink stands ready to join a meet. Some ingenious but uncomfortable seating appears to be made of deer antlers, a popular item for hunting boxes in the mid-Victorian period.

THE BIDDER HOUSE

circa 1865

Height	*50in*	*(127cm) including stand*
Width	*35in*	*(89cm)*
Depth	*17¹/₂in*	*(44cm)*

THIS DOLLS' HOUSE was made for the children of George Bidder (1806–78). He was famous as a very young child as the 'calculating boy', and was exhibited as a mathematical genius from the age of five. More fortunate than many infant prodigies, he grew up to be a distinguished engineer and associate of George Stephenson. The dolls' house was purchased from a descendant. It represents a London house of the period. All the furniture, wallpapers and so forth are original to the house and nothing has been added. Before packing the house, I had the interior photographed and was therefore able to replace the contents exactly as before, even to the plates on the kitchen floor, so that the onlooker is seeing the house exactly as arranged and played with at least 100 years ago. The arrangement of furniture in the past has become a subject of careful study only in the last decade or so, and important and fascinating evidence of this has been thoughtlessly destroyed when dolls'-house furniture was removed for auction or packed away by museums. The dolls formerly in this house of the 1860s were lost or given away. The present ones replaced them and are the usual German dolls'-house dolls. These were made from the same moulds from the 1880s to at least 1914 and possibly later.

A bedroom or night nursery. This pink-papered room is rather sparsely furnished with German furniture. The maid holds a baby; perhaps this is not a very well-run nursery, as the room is distinctly untidy.

Exterior. This is soft wood, painted stone colour with large-scale stucco markings. It has an entrance at the side, up steep steps (the lower ones are missing). There is a working bell pull by the front door, the bell ringing outside at the back of the house. The front opens in two wings.

The hall is decorated in an imitation stone paper (as recommended in decorating books at the time, because if one stone becomes soiled, another may easily be pasted in its place), and the windows are in star-pattern obscured glass. Above the porch roof is a balcony with a balustrade. Despite this realistic entrance, there is no door into the house, and indeed no internal doors or staircases at all.

The bedroom. The wallpaper is a grey seaweed pattern with a narrow gilt fillet which, like other papers in the house, seems to be of an earlier fashion than 1860. The wire-framed half-tester bed is hung with white muslin trimmed with lace. The blue carpet is flat-woven, possibly a piece of a Kidderminster weave. A tinplate hip bath and shower, in cream with black decoration, stand by the fireplace. The furniture is German, including a chest of drawers in the dark mottled-wood finish. Also German is the turned wooden toilet set with floral decoration. On the table is a small, lidless fitted case for toilet things, handmade of cardboard. 127

The drawing room. This is a finely decorated room, the wallpaper with tiny gilt crosses, with a wide paper frieze/border of imitation gathered blue ribbon, fastened with gilt studs. The flat-woven floral carpet was perhaps made from a border for a curtain. The German metal fireplace has two porcelain figures of a shepherd and shepherdess. At the rear is a black Waltershausen bookcase with gilt-transfer decoration of two naked figures reading and writing. Inside are dummy books, and a gilt brass clock is on the top. Other furniture includes a Waltershausen sewing table, a vitrine in the dark mottled finish and a pedestal table with a floral hand-painted top. The sofa and chairs are in German soft pewter. A blonde lady doll admires a bisque dog with puppies.

The kitchen. The ceilings on this semi-basement floor are noticeably lower than the main rooms above. The walls of the kitchen are a simple wood grain, and the floor appears to be covered in floor-cloth or perhaps Kamptulicon, both predecessors of linoleum. It is crowded with rather over-scale tinplate pieces, including a meat screen with a clockwork jack and two Dutch ovens. There is also a quantity of turned wooden ware, dinner plates and so on, and a carpet sweeper.

The dining room. The wallpaper is an arsenical green seaweed pattern, with narrow borders top and bottom in green and gold. The ceiling also has a gilt border, and is centred with a green 'rose' from which hangs a pewter chandelier. The floor has a red flat-woven fitted carpet. There is a pink upholstered sofa and side chairs in dark wood with bulbous legs – these would be more suited to a drawing room. The table groans under a large porcelain dinner-service, and a butler surveys a lady and gentleman on the sofa. On the wall is an early twentieth-century telephone. At the rear on the mantelpiece is a pair of porcelain figurines. On the left is a Waltershausen cabinet with shelves above, supported by bone pillars, acting as a sideboard and containing a very fine set of Continental miniature glass bottles, with ribbed bodies and gilt stems.

129

The nursery. Another low-ceilinged room, but with a pretty paper and serviceable carpet. Apart from the impressive piano, on which a piece titled 'Good Night' is waiting to be played, the furniture is hardly visible for a crowd of girls and boys, together with their governess, who points to a globe. Four of the children are glass-eyed bisque dolls in original clothes; another little girl sports an 'ermine' muff, cape and trimming.

130

THE ORIGINAL SWAN

1865–70

Height	*64in*	*(163cm) including stand*
Width	*38in*	*(97cm)*
Depth	*22¹/₂in*	*(57cm)*

T HIS HOUSE WAS BOUGHT from a lady in Abingdon in Oxfordshire in a derelict state and converted into a pub with rooms. It was quite a feature-less dolls' house but with movable sash windows and a good staircase. There were no wallpapers or fireplaces. It has been arranged as a plain country hotel in a small market town in 1880, catering for farmers and travellers by train. The name was taken from a public house in Cowley, Oxford. The bar, with mirrored overmantel and so on, and frosted glass in the window have been added. Note the stuffed trout in the bar, made by that wonderful craftsman, the late Brown-Morrison of Finderlee. He lived quietly in a basement flat in Brighton when I knew him, but did a great deal of work for the millionaire collector Getty.

The house is back-opening. The front façade is marked to represent stonework or stucco, and the building has been painted yellow. Over the front door, under the portico with the swan, it is displayed that one 'H. G. Greene' is licensed to sell beer, wines and spirits, and tobacco to be consumed on the premises. The real Henry Graham Greene was not aware of his redeployment to a less prestigious occupation.

Because the house is back-opening, we see the cellar under the stairs rather than the front hall.

The parlour. The furniture is largely late nineteenth-century German oak and yellow cherry. There are two framed steel engravings, possibly after Turner, and a vase of dried flowers in the grate. The carpet is floral, and there is an aspidistra on the marble-topped centre table, as well as a copy of *The Graphic* for 23 January 1887.

The bedroom. A brass bedstead is in the centre of the room, the other furniture being a mixture of German oak and cherry. There is a gilt brass clock on the chest of drawers and a white china toilet set with a gilt line. The pictures are photographs of cats and a photogravure picture of an angel taking a child to heaven. The proprietor's family have clearly been to Durham and Madeira at some time, as their labelled trunk is on the carpet.

The dining room. This rather bleak room is perhaps rarely used by visitors. It is furnished with a Schneegas cherrywood dining table and sideboard, and four fretwork chairs in faded red silk. The pictures include a steel engraving of lions, rather a favourite subject of mine, and a Pre-Raphaelite photogravure. A gong and a table bell are evident.

The bar. This is well furnished, with a specially made mahogany bar, crates of bottles and some stoneware jugs, and provided with a handsome barman. There is some old patterned linoleum on the floor, and from the lack of seating, this is not a bar for those in search of a quiet atmosphere. The posters advertise sales of livestock.

THE SHOOTING LODGE

circa 1870

Height	*31in*	*(79cm)*
Width	*23in*	*(58cm)*
Depth	*18in*	*(46cm)*

THIS IS A DECORATIVE MODEL CASTLE rather than a dolls' house, with an exterior in painted stonework. It is similar to the hunting boxes built in the medieval style, under the general influence of Sir Walter Scott, in the Scottish Highlands during the nineteenth century, but this was found in Ireland. There is a sunken pitched roof behind the battlements. The windows, which are far too large for a genuine fortress, are in various coloured glass, which looks effective when lit.

The inside, which can be reached through the main gate or a cupboard door at the side, is set with light metal furniture for a shooting picnic. The ladder staircase is apparently original.

SHELL VILLA

1870–75

Height	*30¹/₂in*	*(77cm)*
Width	*34¹/₂in*	*(88cm)*
Depth	*25in*	*(64cm)*

HERE WE VISIT A LODGING HOUSE for cats in need of sea air, kept by Tabitha, Selina and Branwell Twitchett. Most of the furniture came with the house, which was formerly owned by the Oxford historian A.J.P. Taylor. Cats, new wallpaper and accessories have been added since.

Outside are lobster pots and seaweed (for predicting the weather). The house, which opens in one wing, also has an open back. It has been painted in cheerful seaside colours. A sign points 'To the Esplanade' and a notice in one window offers 'Refined board residence available. Apply within, the Misses Twitchett'.

There are five rooms, hall, staircase and landing. The fifth room is invisible at the back and is empty. The staircase rises sideways at a steep angle. Most of the furniture is 1:15 scale, a little small for the house.

The bedroom. The washstand and other pieces are German 'satinwood' in the style of the 1880s, and a rosewood Waltershausen wardrobe stands at the back. There are gilt candle sconces either side of the mantelpiece.

The landing. The curved banisters are in metal with a cutout pattern. The tinplate jardinière has the trademark of Kindler and Briel, Böblingen, a major German factory for metal and wooden toys which still survives (tradename Kibri). In front is an inspiring statue of Dick Whittington.

The second bedroom. In this rose-patterned room a Miss Twitchett works at the sewing machine, and there is more of the blond wood furniture.

The dining room. The Twitchett family in residence. Alas, Branwell seems to be following the example of his namesake and has taken to drink. A green-glass decanter stands on the oak sideboard and an oil lamp hangs from the ceiling rose.

SHELL VILLA

The drawing room. Here an elegant visitor in hat and muff admires the bronze Viennese bust of a lady cat. The oval table with fitted red-felt cloth with a blue edging is laid for tea. The cherrywood secretaire is German.

Like a typical country vicarage of the period, with a strong Tudor revival influence, then fashionable, the house is extremely well made, with gabled slate roofs and tall Tudor chimneys. The brickwork is carefully outlined and the stonework details, including quoining, windows and so on, are painted buff. Note the Jacobean dog-leg staircase and the hood moulds over the windows. The house is constructed in two halves, hinged at the centre, and the hinged stand was evidently made for it. Houses on this pattern were moderately popular in the late nineteenth century; designs were issued for a basically similar house in the magazine *Amateur Work* in the 1880s. A very strange feature is that there is no front door, although it would have been quite possible to provide one.

144

ST FAITH'S

A Victorian Vicarage *circa* 1870

Height   31in   (79cm) excluding stand
Width   38¹/₂in (98cm)
Depth   29in   (74cm)

Nonie and Faith Rowntree of York, sisters, became collectors after reading my first book and asked me to buy for them the next house I saw, which was this. I always loved it, and when Faith died in 1977 she bequeathed it.

The reader will like to know that little Lily, recently orphaned, has come to live at the vicarage with her aunt (her mother's sister) and her uncle, the vicar. The family is thus in mourning attire. Her trunk is in the hall, and she sits beneath a daguerreotype of her mother. Note the black-edged mourning notepaper on the roll-topped desk. The usual time for children to wear mourning at this period was 'For a parent, 7 months in deep mourning, 6 months in crêpe, 3 months slight'. Underwear was threaded in black ribbon as late as 1910.

The morning room. Here poor Lily sits on an upright settee, part of a suite of 'Old German'-style oak furniture, with a family album for amusement. Above to the left is a daguerreotype of her late mother. The wallpaper is a plain gold, above which is a deep frieze, unexpectedly hand-painted with naked cherubs. Gold paper, considered to be a warm background for the brighter colours in pictures, was fashionable in artistic interiors of this period. The fireplace is an elaborate filigree pewter, from the old-established firm of Babette Schwiezer of Diessen, which is still producing similar items.

Inside the hall is a false front door. The furniture belongs to the house and is very mixed, some dating from about 1890 but most twentieth century. There are a few 1860 pieces. The wallpapers are original, but the curtains (modern) have been removed for ease of viewing in the Rotunda museum. The dolls also came with the house, but were mostly naked and have been redressed.

The interior contains twelve rooms, although some of them could be considered as double-depth rooms, with half in each part of the house, and decorated similarly: for example, the kitchen. There are no internal doors, but although the features – for example, the staircase – are very realistic, this omission does not immediately strike the viewer.

The study. Here Lily's uncle, the vicar, is seated, listening patiently to another younger clergyman. The fireplace is plaster, and there is a large, serious parish desk. The decor is unusual and striking: above the gold wallpaper is a deep frieze showing comic scenes of medieval life in bright colours, the effect being of a room decorated by the Pre-Raphaelites or William Burges.

The schoolroom. This I furnished entirely, and added the bisque girl and boy who sit at a varnished table with bulbous legs. There is a guard in front of the fire. Teaching aids are slates (made for me), books, a globe and a map hanging on the wall. This is not of the world, but of small islands in the Hebrides, 'Rhum, Eigg and Canna'. At the back of the room are two German unvarnished-wood bedside tables with black transfer-printed decoration.

147

The lower hall. Here the vicar's wife descends the stairs, coming to greet her niece in the next room, while Lily's trunk awaits being taken upstairs. The uncarpeted, varnished staircase is finely detailed, with turned spindles and newel post. The wallpaper is cream with a leafy pattern, and a separate paper on the staircase wall is a larger blue leafy pattern. The front door, as mentioned above, is a false one. The long-case clock with a pendulum visible through a glass door seems to be of the Art Déco period.

The landing. The wallpaper has a fashionable deep frieze. The stag's head bears the inscription 'Shot in the Forest of Zenda' – perhaps the vicar's son had a Ruritanian holiday.

THE CARPENTER'S COTTAGE

1880

Height   15¹/₂in   (39cm)
Width   22in   (56cm)
Depth   15¹/₂in   (39cm) including front garden

T HIS SMALL-SCALE COTTAGE, with its little front garden enclosed by a paling fence, is especially attractive for its neatly drawn brickwork covered with a layer of toffee-coloured crackled varnish. I gave it this name, as I felt it was typical of the early artisan cottages of the London suburbs.

It is a back-opening house, which means that we see the staircase which rises from the front hall only on its underside, an unusual view. Under the stairs are stored the mangle, etc.

There are four rooms.

Top left: bedroom 1. This is furnished with modern toy pieces, including a metal bed and a rocker.

Top right: bedroom 2. This has an old lithographed chair and modern toy furniture, including a Barton's chest of drawers from the 1950s. Perhaps a guest bedroom, seldom used, but the housewife's pride and joy.

Lower left: the kitchen This has a German tin and pewter fireplace, a small bisque doll and some modern pieces.

Lower right: the parlour. In here are two small red-covered German armchairs, a lithographed table and chair, and a small-scale Waltershausen piano. Waltershausen furniture was sometimes made in up to nine different sizes, from this size to pieces that would suit a large doll.

CAIRNGORM CASTLE

REPRESENTING 1870–80

Height at tower	*46in*	*(117cm)*
Width	*57in*	*(145cm)*
Depth	*14in*	*(36cm)*

THIS IS THE ONLY EXAMPLE in this collection of a made-up dolls' house. It was seen on a scrap merchant's lorry many years ago, a long narrow house with interesting windows and crenellations. It was bought on the spot, and a tower added by a gifted craftsman, Mr John Gardner. After many years as a fairy palace, painted pink with a roof covered in shells, it was sold. In Christmas week 1991, it appeared in the saleroom. When acquired, a conical roofing was added, and it was redecorated and refurnished. It now represents a wealthy industrialist's idea of a Scottish baronial castle, with a profusion of tartan and all the additions necessary to Highland sport – guns, fishing rods and the company of like-minded friends. Glimpses of this enthusiasm to possess a Highland retreat are to be found in Anthony Trollope's novel *The Eustace Diamonds*. The taste for the Highlands had, of course, been fuelled by Scott's novels and the enthusiasm of Queen Victoria and Prince Albert for Balmoral. Here we see the castle brightly lit, but the original would have been shadowy, with oil lamps and candles only in the bedrooms, and outside the swirling mist.

The drawing room. In this room with its tartan wallpaper and 'The Monarch of the Glen' over the fireplace, the Laird, an imposing figure in tweeds and Glengarry, greets his brother, who commands a Highland regiment and has served in India, Egypt and Abyssinia.

The castellated house has six rooms but no stairs. The landings can be glimpsed only from the main rooms.

Top left: the bathroom. This tower room is furnished in panelled wood, stained as oak, a modern reproduction as in much of the castle. On the floor is a miniature tapestry, of a kind still sold as souvenirs of Cracow Castle in Poland.

Top centre: the bedroom. The polar bear rug is a rabbit skin.

Top right: the landing and drawing room. This has a handsome real marble fireplace with a bust of Lord Beaconsfield on the mantelshelf. Near to the cosy fire sits the widowed mother of the Laird, with a solemn cat on her lap. Alas, her previous pet has been stuffed and placed in a glass case. Her knitting and her cat fill her days, for she takes no part in the housekeeping, being nearly 60, a 'good age' in those days. Tartan covers the floors, seating and walls, but unfortunately the pattern was put up diagonally, so failing in matters of correctness.

Lower left: the study. Two gentlemen discuss field sports, among guns and fishing equipment. The bookcase significantly lacks any reading matter.

Lower centre: the dining room. A buffet lunch has been arranged for the returning sportsmen. On the wall is a stuffed fish.

Lower right: the lounge hall. The leather sofa is battered, and hunting trophies and armour decorate the wall.

JUBILEE

1880–85

Height   60in   (152cm)
Width   45¹/₂in   (116cm)
Depth   22in   (56cm)   *excluding steps*

THIS DOLLS' HOUSE dates from the early 1880s. It was built by a carpenter at Wisbech, Cambridgeshire, to special order, and given to Rhoda Mary Prankherd by her mother. Rhoda's grandmother, Mrs Mary Anne Collins, made all the woolwork carpets herself. Rhoda died in 1913, at the birth of her only child, and her daughter was brought up by her grandmother and played with the dolls' house. Rhoda's half-sister, later Mrs Dolly Button, was never allowed to play with it. The house was presented by Mrs Galloway, Elstree Lodge, Elstree, in Hertfordshire, who one day telephoned quite unexpectedly to offer it. I have made many additions to the original furnishings which came with the house. Some modern items have been added: for instance, the cuckoo clock in the nursery, the dolls' house (American commercial) and the stereoscope (English amateur). The wallpapers are original, except the red wallpaper in the dining room, papered over another, and the *Hobbies* paper in the nursery.

The house retains some decorations, which I added, in celebration of queen Victoria's Jubilee in 1887. It is neatly made, with a shallow-pitched roof, brickwork and two bay windows, unusually on the first not the ground floor. There is a four-panelled front door and the house opens in two wings.

A German pewter filigree bed, complete with home-made mattress and bolster trimmed with red.

153

There are six rooms and a hall, staircase and landings. The stairs, with a late Victorian steepness, have woolwork staircarpet. The wallpaper is cream and shiny, a 'sanitary' paper.

The bedroom. The wallpaper is a brown-edged leaf design and the carpet is original. The furniture is late nineteenth century, from the Schneegas factory in Waltershausen, a bed and two chairs. There is an English mahogany washstand and a marble-topped table with a swing mirror. The tinplate hot-water can has 'Rhoda Mary Prankherd' in pencil on the side; perhaps she wrote it herself.

The night nursery. The wallpaper is a pale-blue diaper design, and the carpet a geometric woolwork, one of many made by Rhoda's grandmother. Here stands a bisque little girl with an Alice band, next to a baby in a cot, while the nursery maid is washing another baby in a hip bath. Note the jug and basin in a circular pewter stand. The bed is a German blond wood half-tester.

The day nursery. Here a dramatic scene takes place. As the governess enters, exercise book in hand, one little girl is distraught and the other lies on the floor in a tantrum, while nanny raises her hands in horror. The cause of all this appears to be the spilt milk on the floor, which the kittens are lapping up. The room has a 1920s dolls'-house nursery paper with a frieze of animals, and the carpet is original. There is a scrap screen and an early upright piano, probably English. On the wall at the back are some bright lithographs of children in gilt frames.

The kitchen. This has a woodgrain wallpaper and is laid with linoleum. Unlike most British kitchens of this period, it is well equipped, with an American cast-iron stove and a central-heating boiler. At the back on the left I have added an antique yellow-glazed pottery butler's sink. An over-realistic touch is the fly paper, black with (bead) flies.

The dining room. This has been repapered in a bold red, with a drapery frieze, and the carpet is red and blue woolwork. The dark wood sofa and five chairs are in red velvet to match. The fireplace is a tinplate one made by the famous German toymaker Märklin. On the mantelpiece is a Waltershausen clock, and a (modern) case of medals hangs on the wall to the left. The butler presides over a table laid with onion-pattern porcelain; the meal is cold salmon and fruit, with a ham on the sideboard. Also on the table is a glass and gilt German pewter stand for oil and vinegar (see opposite).

The oil and vinegar stand
from the dining room table.

The drawing room.
Here is another
family gathering; the
soldier is seated on
the couch because he
has been wounded.
Commiserating with
him are a blonde
bisque lady and
gentleman, and an
earlier china lady. The
two little girls are a
glass-eyed bisque of
the late nineteenth
century and a much
earlier 1860 china
clasping her own doll.
Both the wallpaper
and the carpet are
original, with
geometric patterns.
The fireplace is
unusual, made in
polished steel, with an
alabaster clock and a
Parian figure under a
dome on the
mantelpiece. Just
visible on the wall to
the right is a tiny
German cuckoo clock,
with hanging weights.
On the vitrine at the
back is a Parian bust
of Queen Victoria,
to commemorate
the Jubilee.

157

The house, which is dated 1886 over the front door, is well built and professionally made. It is on a wide, flat base with steps to the front door and the shallow-pitched roof is slated with two chimneys. At the left side of the house are three bay windows and at the rear is a long Gothic window, extending through the first and second storeys and casting a multicoloured gloom on the staircase. The scored brickwork is painted a dark red and the stonework cream. At the back of the house is a rain-water hopper and downpipe; unfortunately there are no gutters. The front of the house is in three sections.

On the Waltershausen sewing table in the students' room is a very tiny ivory chessboard with its red and white men.

IVY LODGE

1886

Height 58in (147cm)
Width 54in (137cm)
Depth 20in (51cm)

THIS HOUSE WAS ACQUIRED in Sussex. I named it Ivy Lodge, but it is perhaps misnamed, for I imagined it as a typical north Oxford house. It belongs to an Oxford tutor, the Reverend Compton-Burnett, a widowed clergyman who lives here with his two daughters and two undergraduate lodgers, one of whom is evidently a medical student and the other, I think, reads history. The tutor, in his gown, is correcting papers in his study, and the President of Trinity gave me part of a discarded gown of his to dress the doll appropriately. The finest possible needle would hardly piece the black silk. It was not that the fabric was thick, but it was so closely woven that hand-sewing on so small a scale was almost impossible. The daughters are both dressed in material at least 100 years old; the child in mourning had to be made entirely by myself, and I was delighted to find that the minute black beads in a Victorian workbox were exactly the right size for the child's black boots.

The housekeeper's room. There is no kitchen in this house; even as late as this, kitchens were barely mentioned in books on interior design and decoration. This rather shabby room has whitewashed walls and a jaspé linoleum floor, with a rag rug. The housekeeper, in her black dress, with scissors hanging from a chatelaine, sits on a chintz armchair, with a matching squashy sofa. Her tea kettle hangs above the spirit stove and a cut cake decorated with whole strawberries, is on the tea-table. A carpet beater, a carpet sweeper and a stepladder show this is also a storeroom, and an ivory mouse ignores the cat in the basket.

There are six rooms, plus a central hall and two landings. All the wallpapers are original but the furniture has been added. The staircase, the floor with scored floorboards and the doors on the landings are excellently made in mahogany, with elaborate newel posts and banisters in the Gothic style. A lady in a riding habit has slung her saddle carelessly over the newel post in the hall. At the rear glows the long window with its Gothic tracery and red, green, blue and yellow glass, evoking the comfortable piety of north Oxford in the 1880s.

The dining room. The wallpaper is a fashionable, 'aesthetic', gold-embossed paper, thought to provide a fine setting for pictures, and the carpet is paisley. The dining table is laid for a light collation of cake and fruit, supervised by the butler and a housemaid. The hideous epergne on the table is modelled with deer. The dining chairs are English mahogany with cut-velvet seats (the matching settee is in the hall). The sideboard is oak, with decanter and glasses, and the long-case clock is a finely made miniature piece.

The study. The wallpaper is a shiny, embossed imitation leather in green and red with formal sprays of pink flowers. The Reverend Compton-Burnett works at his plain German secretaire, while a younger cleric sits with a cat on his knee by the fire. The mantelpiece is crowded with ornaments, and a Parian bust of the widowed Queen stands in the corner. On the rear wall is a small early Victorian romantic oil painting of a lady. Lying on the table are a pair of gilt spectacles and a copy of the *Evening News* for 18 October 1886.

The drawing room.
The wallpaper is yellow, scattered with bouquets of violets, and has a gilt border. The two daughters of the family, in elegant mauve and blue silk dresses, greet a widowed friend and a little orphan girl. Another lady visitor has a beige costume corded in brown, with a matching cape, real fur muff and a black hat with a red ribbon. The furniture includes some fashionable gilt pieces, including two chairs which started life as needlecases made by Avery, the needlemakers. At the back is a modern piece, a post-war Szalasi chair in Baroque style. There is a gilt brass firescreen and table, and a gilt china clock. The Japanese craze was then at its height, and a fan and two paper sunshades are hanging on the wall.

The bedroom. Here stands a bisque lady in a ruffled blue dress with beige and black lace. The fireplace is marbled and inside it stands a smaller Evans and Cartwright fireplace. The marbled wallpaper is an unusual pattern. Two oval gilt brass frames hang on the rear wall and on the right wall is a pewter frame with candleholders at each side, for a devotional picture. There is a dark wooden bed and a Waltershausen rosewood dressing table, with an old miniature tin of toilet powder. This is only 1in (2.5cm) high, but is minutely printed with the following words:

> Cherry Blossom Toilet Powder lends a charm to existence. Certificate showing that climate causes no chemical changes:–
>
>   John Gosnell Co.'s toilet powder, Calcutta Medical College, 23 July 1880. I have examined chemically and microscopically the contents of a packet of toilet and nursery powder prepared by John Gosnell Co. London, and from that I find that it consists of perfumed starch and is free from all admixture of injurious mineral or vegetable matter.
>
> C. H. J. Warden
Chemical Examiner to Government

On the washstand is a fine china jug and basin, and beside it is a yellow tinplate hot-water can. On the cherrywood marble-topped chest of drawers is a brass toilet mirror.

On the hall table are two old parcels which have never been opened, with miniature labels marked 'William Whiteley, Universal Providers, Westbourne Grove' and 'Peter Robinson, Oxford St. & Regent St.'.

The students' room. Here the two undergraduates are at ease with a friend with sideburns who has just come in from a tennis match. His costume was copied from an illustration in *Punch.* Of the others, the one with the moustache in a dressing jacket is at his desk and the bearded friend in a suit of loud checks relaxes in a rocking chair. Both these costumes are original. Note the college oar and the smoking cap on the wall, and the articulated skeleton. There is something very disagreeable preserved in a tall bottle – I dare not guess what it is. The furniture includes Japanese-style black bentwood chairs and sofa, a Waltershausen desk with pewter decorative trim and a Waltershausen sewing table. The wallpaper has blue flowers and leaves on a white ground.

There are only two rooms; such houses rarely have stairs, although occasionally there are lifts!

The original decorative wallpapers, pasted in bordered panels with a narrow frieze, represent a late, simplified version of the French *décor* papers mentioned in relation to Regency Gothick (see pages 72–9) and there are also typical tiled floor papers. The two rooms are furnished with German cherrywood furniture of about the same period as the house, with rather fussy turnings. The asymmetrical piece in the centre of the living room seems to show influences from Japanese and Art Nouveau styles. There are two gilt brass candlesticks and two French penny toys, a little table and a dressing table in metal alloy. Penny toys of this kind were mass-produced in France at the turn of the century and later, by firms such as Simon and Rivollet of Paris; they have found a place in the smallest dolls' house.

THE FOLLY

1880–90

Height   *33in*   *(84cm)*
Width   *19¹/₂in (50cm)*
Depth   *16in*   *(40cm)*

T HIS RECENTLY ACQUIRED small "blue-roof" German villa of the late nineteenth century is the only non-British house in the collection. Underneath the house is a pencilled number 2115. This identifies it as one of the very long sequence of numbered houses made by Moritz Gottschalk of the small town of Marienberg in Saxony, Germany, a firm founded in 1867 and in existence long enough to celebrate its centenary in 1967, though it was taken into state control by the East German government and subsequently closed. Owing to post-war lack of contact with East Germany, the origins of these houses were unknown to Western collectors and in many older books they are described as 'French'. It was not until 1982, when the editor of this book published a 1926 advertisement of this firm in *International Dolls' House News*, that the maker was identified and serious research began.

A recent book, *The Genius of Moritz Gottschalk*, by American writer and collector Evelyn Ackerman, includes on page 35 illustrations of an almost identical house, No. 2114. Such differences as there are, apart from size (2115 is larger), may be attributed either to losses (2114 has lost its garden walls and probably the panels beneath the ground-floor windows), to repainting (2115 has suffered some alterations to the paint-work) or to minor renovation. The pinnacles of the central tower differ in detail.

The special attraction of Gottschalk houses lies in the use of brightly coloured chromo-lithographed papers, inside and out, to represent architectural and decorative details, and it was this feature, both cheap to produce and eye-catching, that ensured their commercial success. However, the earlier houses, such as this one, have a greater wealth of applied wooden details and mouldings than the later examples. This house is papered externally with lithographed brick above and stone below. The central pointed tower, intended no doubt to remind us of an old *Schloss* or château, is made separately. The blue roof was intended to indicate slate tiles, a common feature of nineteenth-century houses in the highlands of Saxony. Villas of this type were common in Germany and Continental Europe in the late nineteenth century, and would probably have been considered by their middle-class owners as romantic and luxurious rather than eccentric.

The interior shows an opulent decor, with a central staircase dividing at a half-landing into two parallel flights up to the first-floor landing. There is much use of mirror. The family of dolls is celebrating the wedding of their daughter; I made all the dresses and uniforms from materials of the period, and also the flowers and the wedding cake. The bride's dress is of tulle and satin, embroidered in silver thread, the material dating to 1870. She wears a necklace of real seed pearls.

168

THE CEDARS, WOODBRIDGE

LATE NINETEENTH CENTURY

Height	*29in*	*(74cm)*
Width	*36¹/₂in*	*(93cm)*
Depth	*26¹/₂in*	*(67cm)*

T HIS HOUSE IS FROM SUFFOLK, apparently from the late nineteenth century, but evidently specially made and beautifully finished in an earlier idiom. It has been repapered and provided with furniture of 1865–70.

The exterior seeks a solution to the problem of a house with a realistic interior and constructed with a double layer of rooms. The front façade opens in two wings, and on the left side an opening near the back of the house gives access to the pantry and day nursery. Through the pantry at the back of the house lies the kitchen, barely accessible and not visible. On the right side, the big drawing room on the ground floor, with its elegant bay window with bowed glass, extends to the back of the house. Above this, a small opening gives access to the night nursery. In the mansard roof, behind the row of windows, are the servants' bedrooms, which have not been furnished.

THE CEDARS, WOODBRIDGE

The pantry. This tiny room, with wood-grain paper, is used for storing glass, china and so on. A glimpse of the inaccessible kitchen can be seen through the door.

The reception room. This fine drawing room, extending the depth of the house, and seeming larger with the effect of a mirror on the rear wall, is crowded with the wedding party, apparently just getting ready to cut the cake. The bride is a statuesque figure beside her plump, black-haired groom, who has a moustache. One male relative is in scarlet regimentals and the older ladies have impressive hats. A small boy at the front is clearly concerned only with the photographer, who must be capturing this scene for posterity. Waltershausen furniture, and the pewter music-stand with music for a mazurka (right), are almost unnoticeable in the crowd, although the glass chandelier, with white glass candles set in frilly blue-glass holders, can be picked out.

The day nursery. Here a nurserymaid looks after the baby. A gilt-framed picture shows a scrap of children playing with a snowman.

The bride's bedroom. Here the maidservant is packing the bride's clothes for going away. Her trunk lies open on the floor, with her corsets on the top layer, and the maid is holding an embroidered nightdress. On the bed lies her silver-embroidered evening dress. Suitably opulent furniture includes a Gothic revival Waltershausen chest of drawers with a marble top and a marble-topped washstand, on which is part of the turned wooden toilet set. The bed is a draped half-tester, and at the back is a fine-quality miniature fruitwood wardrobe (far left), which has a surprise: in the right cupboard is a night commode!

On a chest in the second bedroom is a set of W.H. Goss miniature china jugs and basin. Goss is famous for its china cottages and souvenir ware, but also made fine-quality miniatures.

THE EDWARDIAN VILLA

circa 1905

Height	29in	(74cm)	
Width	45in	(116cm)	excluding base
Depth	25¹/₂in	(65cm)	excluding base

THIS HOUSE WAS BOUGHT derelict and I furnished it, partly with late Victorian and Edwardian furniture and partly with 'fun' pieces specially made for the house – the geyser, the gas globe, the mahogany lavatory and wash basin and so on. It was obviously made as a unique piece. It is very elaborate, with a double depth of rooms and façades on both sides. The building is on the rough side, but with a multitude of features typical of the style Osbert Lancaster christened 'Wimbledon Transitional':

> Two of its most striking features . . . first, the skilful but unrestrained use of white-painted wooden balconies, porches and verandas; second the revival of half-timbering, a method of building which had been allowed to remain in a state of well-merited neglect for nearly three centuries.

Here the architectural profusion includes a conservatory, tall 'Elizabethan' chimneys, bay windows, porthole windows, black and white half-timbering and a turret with a weather-cock.

There is access on both sides of he house, and a total of thirteen rooms, including the magnificent hall and the conservatory.

Bedroom 1. The household is preparing for the wedding of a daughter. A dressmaker is fitting the stoutly built lady for an elaborate dress (both are blonde bisque dolls), and her wedding boots lie on the floor. Dresses on stands, a hat and paper patterns litter the room. In the background is a nice gilt pewter German bed.

The rooms at the rear of the house include the lavatory and bathroom and the second bedroom on the upper floor. On the ground floor are the study/larder and a boiler room/kitchen. The boiler room is used to store carpet sweepers and so on, while the kitchen contains blue enamel utensils on a dresser and a maidservant in a white cap and apron.

The drawing room. This opens into the conservatory at the rear. A pale-blue brocade carpet matches pale-blue walls. Two pale-blue silk armchairs are edges in cord and fringe, and there are two red and white striped single chairs, all in pale wood, all late nineteenth century. Lamps include a gilt brass floor-standing oil lamp, and two glass wall lamps with candles each side of the fireplace. In the fireplace is a stuffed peacock, a fashionable decoration at the time.

The lavatory and bathroom. Equipped with specially made mahogany fittings, boxed in as was then the fashion, to be revived in the nostalgic 1980s. Old pieces include a pewter oil heater and a circular, white wooden wash-hand basin.

The hall. The grandiose hall has a fine staircase dividing on to two galleries. Under the staircase are pillared arches, a popular feature at that date (known as 'Liberty Arches', because they could be purchased at Liberty's shop). The banisters are elaborately turned. On the rear wall is a large pipe organ; it does not have a keyboard but is powered by a musical box! At the front is a German carved wooden bear, a feature still popular at the time and often used to hold a lamp, a bearskin rug, suits of armour and hunting trophies.

MODEL HOUSES

Model houses were made as decorative objects rather than as toys in both the eighteenth and nineteenth centuries. Sometimes they also had a useful function; for example, as watch holders at a time when there was a tax on clocks. Some were made in the home, following designs published in magazines, and others were commercial fancy articles or souvenirs. Many incorporated rather fragile materials, such as paper, mica, shells and moss, and these were usually kept under glass domes or in cases. Sometimes a garden is added, and in France elaborate scenes incorporating Nevers glass figures were constructed. Those in this collection are quite small and simple, all less than 12in (30cm) high, and were all probably originally under glass.

Top left: A cottage covered in shells and coarse sand, probably a souvenir piece.

Top right: A little Victorian Gothic house, with fretwork bargeboards and window frames.

Bottom left: Another shellwork cottage, with a tiled roof.

Bottom right: 'Darwin House', a strange little home-made cottage with a curved awning over the upper window and a paper tree stuck on one side.

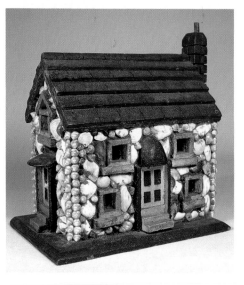

FURNITURE

This furniture is part of a separate collection in cabinets at the Rotunda, and does not form part of the contents of any specific house.

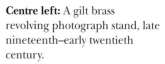

Top left: A group of nineteenth-century small pieces in carved bone, including a table with a filigree top, an elaborate chess table with red and white bone pieces, a potty chair (with a china baby) and a cricket cage. Turned and fretted bone pieces were made as part of a souvenir industry in Germany, at, among other places, Berchtesgaden and Geislingen. Some pieces came also from the Far East and it is difficult to pin down the origin of each.

Top right: A French porcelain cabaret set, gilt-edges and with a rose pattern. This set is marked Limoges; similar items were made by other factories in the Paris area.

Centre left: A gilt brass revolving photograph stand, late nineteenth–early twentieth century.

Centre right: Two gilt brass wall lamps with electric fittings, German, early twentieth century.

Bottom left: A Waltershausen wardrobe, finished in black with a gilt transfer design showing a romantic cavalier delivering a letter to a lady. Themes of this kind were popular, based on the novels of Scott and German Romantic writers, in the early nineteenth century.

Bottom right: A mahogany 'thunder-box' (portable closet), with a porcelain knob to tilt the basin, nineteenth century.

FURNITURE

Top left: A gilt pewter firescreen, with a piece of silk embroidery, of the type made by the Schweizer firm, Diessen, Germany.

Top centre: A gilt brass pendulum clock, late nineteenth century.

Top right: Hanging shelves made in pewter, with mirrored back, German, nineteenth century.

Centre left: A splendid gilt brass chandelier with electric fittings, *c.* 1900. Working electric fittings for dolls' houses were available, as were those for model trains, before they were at all common in ordinary homes.

Centre: A pewter firescreen with a lithophane insert, German, late nineteenth century. At the back is a candle holder; when illuminated, the glass lithophane shows a picture with a three-dimensional effect.

Centre right: A gilt brass parrot-stand with bird. Note the tray to collect droppings!

Bottom left: A group of green glass, including an English bottled beer, a bottle of Malaga wine and a German cake-stand with pewter frame, offering a selection of jam tarts.

Bottom right: An early nineteenth-century French brass clock, about one inch (2.4cm) high, dated 1812. It actually works, but is missing its glass dome.

The Dolls' House and the Historical Treatment of Toys

by Margaret Towner

Children's toys, as part of the general clutter of domestic life, have been on view from the earliest times, but like most aspects of our home surroundings, they had little attention from the writer or historian in the past. They feature very often in portraits of family groups or children, but certainly in the Tudor period and later they are generally introduced for symbolic purposes: the little girl clutches a doll as a token of future motherhood, and the boy holds a toy sword or wears a helmet to indicate a martial tradition. It is in accounts of royalty or nobility that toys are most frequently mentioned in a historical context, since the social status of the owner gives them a unique importance. Most detailed of these accounts is the journal of Jean Heroard, describing the early seventeenth-century childhood of Louis XIII of France, the work of a physician devoted to the service of his young master. Many of the Dauphin's toys are described; a glass water toy which worked a fountain, a sand toy which showed dancing marionettes, toy dinner services and pots and pans. None of these would conceivably have been recorded had they not played a part in the development of this child, whose character would be of vital importance to the future success and prosperity of France.

In England the Protestant tradition resulted in a long period, from the seventeenth century onwards, during which the child was considered almost exclusively as a brand to be saved from the burning, and literature for and about children was principally concerned with keeping them from idleness or sinful occupation. In literature this involved the proscription of romance and fiction, and the prescription of tales of the death and martyrdom of children. There was no place here for the toy, a word which at that period defined any trifling object. When, in the later eighteenth century, philosophers and educationalists increasingly considered the proper management of the child, toys had importance in accordance with whether or not they were felt to have some value in the development of the character or moral values, but it was generally agreed that they should not be expensive or elaborate. Rousseau went so far as to prefer natural objects, such as branches, to manufactured articles.

It was at about the same time, when the virtues of Romantic savagery became fashionable, that the reality of a rising urban middle class in Europe encouraged the development in Germany of industrial toy manufacture. This industry was based on the small-scale rural arts of turning, carving and so on of poor highland areas in Saxony, Thüringia and the Gröden Valley, the last now part of Italy. The commercial centre for the toy trade became established at Nuremberg, which was also a centre of manufacture for metal toys. Soon this industry was to supply nineteenth-century England with immense quantities of goods, including dolls'-house furniture, at all prices and of every quality.

The toy industry became of great importance to the states concerned (Germany not being a unified country until later in the nineteenth century) and was the subject of study by several German writers, mainly from an economic and social viewpoint, since the toymakers suffered increasing exploitation and poverty. There was little or no consideration of the history of the toys themselves, nor were there any books for the general reader, in translation or otherwise, since toys were of no interest to adults. In England the most detailed accounts of the home toy industry occur in the interviews conducted by

Henry Mayhew, the social reformer, as part of his investigations into the livelihood of the poor and deprived in early nineteenth-century London: he deals with dolls and some other toys, but not dolls' houses.

For an interest in dolls' houses, and the ability to capture the interest of the public in them, it is necessary to turn to that most talented of all publicists Charles Dickens. Toys and toymakers became one aspect of his celebration of family life, children and Christmas. Two of his best-known short pieces contain some of the first detailed fictional references to dolls' houses and furniture. *The Cricket on the Hearth* of 1845, 'a fairy-tale of home', is the story of the poor toymaker Caleb and his blind daughter Bertha, and every nuance of the contrast between the wretched family and the gaily painted dolls and toys which surround them is exploited:

> Caleb and his daughter were at work together in their usual working room, which served them for their ordinary living room as well; and a strange place it was. There were houses in it, finished and unfinished, for Dolls of all stations in life. Suburban tenements for Dolls of moderate means; kitchens and single apartments for Dolls of the lower classes; capital town residences for dolls of high estate . . . The nobility and gentry and public in general, for whose accommodation these tenements were designed, lay, here and there, in baskets, staring straight up at the ceiling.

In another short piece of 1845, 'A Christmas Tree', Dicken's acute observation and grasp of detail led him to describe, as decorations for this very fancy tree, 'French-polished tables, chairs, bedsteads, wardrobes, eight-day clocks, and various other articles of domestic furniture (wonderfully made, in tin, at Wolverhampton), perched among the boughs, as if in preparation for some fairy housekeeping'. This little catalogue accurately describes the products of the English toy factory of Messrs Evans and Cartwright of Wolverhampton which, after that one brief recognition, were quite forgotten and remained unrecognized until the late 1980s.

Throughout the nineteenth century the increasing sentimental interest in children, as well as concern for their welfare and happiness, produced a mass of literature for and about them in which toys of all kinds are described and illustrated. Stories about dolls' houses are legion, and the Victorian genre painters, such as Frederick Daniel Hardy, regularly introduced them as props in their scenes of cottage interiors. This eventually awakened some interest in the toys themselves, and more especially in the conditions under which they were produced on the Continent. In 1885 Mrs Brewer, a journalist writing for *The Girl's Own Paper*, went on a trip to the toy-making areas of Germany, and published detailed accounts in that magazine of the products and processes involved, as well as of the lives, often sad, of the workers in the various small towns, Lauscha, Grunhainichen and so on, which were the centres of manufacture of dolls' houses and their accessories. Later, in *The Girl's Realm Annual* for 1901, an article of a similar type appeared on the life of an East London dolls' house-maker, making box-back houses for a large wholesaler, and working a seventeen-hour day.

However, it was in France that the study of toys at last achieved literary respectability. Paris had long been the centre of the trade in luxury toys, especially the porcelain dolls of such firms as Bru and Jumeau. While it also produced attractive but sometimes flimsy toy shops, schools and stables, it apparently had no manufacture of dolls' houses. But Paris was also the location for some of the great international exhibitions, at which the toys and dolls of all nations obtained publicity and attention from the general public. A group of well-to-do Parisians became collectors and connoisseurs of toys, not only of antique pieces from the eighteenth century, but of current production, including the cheap mechanical toys so popular at the turn of the century. They formed a group known as Les Amateurs de Jouets et Jeux and two of their number, among other activities, produced books on the history of toys. Leo Claretie published *Les Jouets* in 1896. Henri René d'Allemagne produced his *Histoire des Jouets* in 1908, a book which, although long out of print, has provided source material for innumerable later writers on the subject. Naturally these writers concentrated on the toy in France, but this was the start of the general literature of toy collecting. D'Allemagne in included a great deal of material on early French model rooms and Nuremberg dolls' houses, although he did not cover English houses.

In 1908, the year that *Histoire des Jouets* appeared, the first English book on the subject, *Toys of Other Days* by Mrs F. Nevill Jackson, was published by *Country Life* magazine. In this book is an account of several of the more important German dolls' houses, including the group of seventeenth-century houses at Nuremberg, an illustration of Queen Victoria's childhood house at Kensington Palace, and a brief mention of modern houses: 'Now, we need hardly say that they are "turned out" by thousands, very pretty and complete they are, but as works of art or examples of fine workmanship in miniature, they need not be discussed.' Despite this dismissive attitude to contemporary production and the omission of any early English houses, this book, with its treatment of antique miniature furniture and fittings, was probably the most useful book on dolls' houses up to the time of Vivien Greene's first publication in 1955. In the intervening period German authors such as Karl Grober and Max von Boehn brought a more scholarly approach to some aspects of toy history. However, the only treatment of English dolls' houses was in occasional articles in *Country Life* by general writers on antiques, such as G. Bernard Hughes and Christopher Hussey, considering a few of the more important baby houses in stately homes.

During the early part of this century, the collection of miniature objects by adults became very fashionable, and the creation of the miniature house at Windsor Castle for Queen Mary and of Titania's Palace by Sir Neville Wilkinson spurred on both the toy industry and individual craftsman to produce new miniatures, many reflecting contemporary conceptions of the Tudor or Georgian past. A number of women began to collect miniature objects and to create miniature rooms, among them Madame Helena Rubinstein, founder of the cosmetics business, and Mrs James Ward Thorne, creator of a series of historic American and European miniature rooms. And then there was that omnivorous collector of every kind of object, Mrs Homer Strong, whose collection of dolls' houses forms a major element of the Strong Museum in Rochester, New York. As far as English houses are concerned, the most discriminating collector before the Second World War was Mrs Mary Greg, whose collection, including many beautiful Georgian baby houses, was left in part to London's Victoria and Albert Museum (The Museum of Childhood, Bethnal Green) and in part to the City of Manchester Museum, which has not had them on general display for about twenty years.

Until the war was over, none of the collectors had attempted anything in the way of serious historical research, and Vivien Greene was on her own in England when she started to study antique dolls' houses, and to compare and categorize those which she tracked down all over Great Britain. While she was engaged in this, another collector, Flora Gill Jacobs of Washington, USA, was at work on her *History of Dolls' Houses*, and they occasionally came across each other's tracks. Mrs Jacobs's first book, published in 1953, was a general study of the subject worldwide, and she later went on to produce the most comprehensive survey of *Dolls' Houses in America*.

The book, which was the result of Vivien Greene's work, *English Dolls' Houses of the Eighteenth and Nineteenth Centuries*, published in 1955, was a *tour de force* of careful observation and analysis. It was followed in 1973 by *Family Dolls' Houses*, a more general work describing a sequence of houses in chronological order, but incorporating a variety of original observations on the character and contents of the houses.

Since 1955 toy-collecting has become a popular hobby, and there have been a large number of useful and important books on various categories of toys and dolls, as well as specialist periodicals devoted to the subject, but none has been more innovative and well researched than *English Dolls' Houses*.

The Development of the English Dolls' House from 1700 to 1900

This is an extract from Vivien Greene's first book, *English Dolls' Houses of the Eighteenth and Nineteenth Centuries*, slightly revised to incorporate research since 1955 and reference to houses in the Collection.

Other books on the dolls' house have traced back its European history to origins in the sixteenth century, and described in detail the magnificent houses created for the nobles and merchants of Germany in the seventeenth century. A group of these can be seen wonderfully preserved in the Germanisches Nationalmuseum in Nuremberg. The immediate inspiration for the early English houses came almost certainly not from Germany but from Holland, in the wake of the Glorious Revolution of 1687, which brought to Britain a Dutch King, William, his English Queen, Mary, and their court. Many aspects of English interior decoration, as well as the layout of gardens, were brought under Dutch influence, and one fashionable feature of wealthy houses in Holland at time was the dolls' house.

Indeed, in Holland a fashion which was almost a rage, reminding us of the tulip mania, seems to have risen among the rich merchants to have reproductions of their own possessions made by craftsmen: even miniature copies of pictures and tapestry, china and plate, were commissioned.

The seventeenth-century dolls' houses in which these miniatures were placed, displayed now in The Hague, Amsterdam and Utrecht, are without façades or staircases, being cabinets, often of magnificent workmanship. They have fine carved stands, and the doors may be inlaid with ivory and decorated with marquetry, having a central opening and a key. The interiors are extremely elaborate, with rooms panelled or tapestried, and always with a top-floor room arranged as a laundry, with charcoal irons on a long table and a drying rack suspended from the ceiling. Piles of blankets lie stacked in a walnut press, jars and barrels line the storeroom: in one house real dried fish, a scoopful of dace or sprats, are threaded on a string on the wall. In one nursery an inch of lace, with its minute bobbins, is pinned half-completed to its pillow, and in a dining room a collection of shells is displayed in a bow cabinet. And always there are the long-bodied dolls, the dark, flat glass glittering in swarthy wax faces, attentive at a curtained bed (the new-born is in cap and robe) or commanding among the copper pots (fowls in a coop await dispatch). There is silverware in the kitchen, and in the library the poker and tongs and the charcoal footwarmer are reproduced in silver, as well as the chocolate pot and tray for the dining room. These 'toys', as they were later called, became a separate craze or fashion, and they were so greatly valued that they were separately specified in wills in the late seventeenth and eighteenth centuries.

The most famous of these houses are the Utrecht dolls' house of 1700, which has an art room filled with fine pictures and ornaments, and the house in the Rijksmuseum made for Petronella Brandt Oortman of 1690–1705. These masterpieces can never have been regarded as playthings for children, but they are authentically dolls' houses as we know them. Yet so splendid a possession must have been a rarity even among those opulent merchants, and perhaps less a personal hobby than an illustrated inventory, a boast of industry, good judgement and taste. There is something formidable about this cabinetwork on its ornate stand, rich and dark as plum cake, suitable to the 'richest and most enlightened trading corporation the world has ever seen'.

The very earliest surviving English baby houses, of the very late seventeenth century – for example, Ann Sharp's baby house, inherited by the Bulwer Long family – are also houses in cabinets. However, they differ from the Dutch examples in their total lack of grandeur; Ann Sharp's cabinet is a plain glazed wooden one, and the interior, although fascinating to a degree, is neither luxurious nor full of fine art. The William and Mary cabinet (see pages 18–19), although its date is not certain, also reflects this comparative simplicity. However, from very early in the eighteenth century, English houses begin to appear with a real façade, with windows and a front door, and sometimes an indicated staircase within, and it is these features which will eventually provide character and importance for the English dolls' house later in the century.

The early examples, *circa* 1700–20, were comparatively small, often of unpainted wood, smoothly polished and deriving in appearance from the Dutch prototype in that the stand was given almost as great an importance as the house. The taller the stand, relatively, the earlier it is (see pages 27–9, the Mahogany House). These early houses usually had fixed fronts, or a fixed panel in the centre of the façade, with each side of the front (or 'wings' as I call them for clarity) opening to right and left, and each wing secured by at least one lock to the panel. With the fixed front is associated the half-staircase, or the few steps giving the effect of a continuous stair. There were never more than four rooms; the whole structure is extremely solid, often of oak. The Georgian House (see pages 24–6) is an example of a house with a fixed front and both sides opening.

By 1730 the façade is richer, though the size remains moderate. From now on the house is painted to represent brick or stone, and carved to show quoining or rustication. The stands are lower and usually quite plain. Then, very suddenly, it seems, by the middle of the century the baby house became both larger and more elaborate. It is now not only too large to lift but too large to move at all. The stand, if any, was often painted to resemble the brickwork or stone of the house, so that imaginatively there is a stable or a watergate below, and no doubt the deep arches might make convenient mooring places for Noah's Ark, or stabling for hobby-horses, when it was permitted to play with the great baby house on the landing. This was the golden age, since when the perfection of detail has never been surpassed. We examine the carved or marbled chimney-pieces, the grates of polished steel, the brass escutcheons of the minute keyholes, the arched niches with shell ornamentation and their curved shelves, 1in (2.5cm) wide. Rooms may be panelled, the mouldings picked out in white or gilt on an olive ground, or they are spread with Chinese wallpaper, exuberant with pheasants and peonies in richest blue, sulphur and pink. A staircase of shallow risers swings lightly from attic to basement. On the sides glimmer rows of windows, glazed, but at the end of the century sometimes backed with pitch on the reverse, a reference to the increased window tax of 1784 (see pages 60–3, the Balustraded House), and these bear pediments above them, while brackets support the sills and balustrading, or urns may decorate the roof above the dentil cornice. Such a house is in pine, sometimes limewood.

Occasionally, a smaller house, no less elaborate, has a contemporary stand, sometimes in Chinese Chippendale style, or with cabriole legs, but the typical house of this period is distinguished for its size (see pages 42–7, Cane End House) and more especially its depth.

As every large baby house was individually made, it is extremely unwise to make a hard and fast assertion, and this outline of a trend is based on my own tentative dating of about 1,500 English examples, some very dilapidated and many evidently country-made. This means they lag behind the current mode in architecture, as much as did the more sophisticated estate carpenter who, when commissioned to make a baby house, may have taken as his model the nearest large house, his employer's. In spite of the extraordinary number of country houses built in the mid-eighteenth century, such a house must often have been put up a generation or two earlier. Can it not, then, be assumed of a baby house that it is not a copy but a reminiscence of an earlier building? The posy 'It is later than you think' particularly applies to the dating of a house. This might in part explain why so many houses were formerly described as 'Queen Anne'; her short reign of twelve years could not conceivably have produced the number asserted to have been made before 1714. And again, in the next century, pediments, of strange proportions certainly, were given to dolls' houses made in the 1860s and 1870s – that is, at a time when one would suppose the Palladian as a domestic style to be completely moribund.

By the 1800s it is perfectly clear that the baby house is no longer commissioned and furnished chiefly by adults for adult amusement. It has lost that 'valuable' appearance and a decisive difference in aim is apparent; it has become a nursery plaything. There may have been one of those undocumented changes of taste, as when young women ceased to 'drizzle' and became enchanted with netting purses, until that in its turn gave way to beadwork. In the same way, it appears that the baby house ceased to amuse the elders of a family, although beautiful *petit point* carpets and painted fire-screens were made, as records testify, in the 1830s and 1840s by kindly aunts for the children's plaything, but the miniature silver had long been replaced by china, pottery and turned woodware; cornices and panelling disappear, the houses are well proportioned and large, but now they are convenient to play with (see pages 80–4, Durward's Hall). The front opens in one piece or in two, and above all – and this marks the change of status more than anything else – the locks have disappeared. From the inlaid cabinet of the seventeenth century, with its furnished rooms, down to the beginning of the nineteenth century, every house had the potential of being filled with precious things. Now, suddenly, we find it merely hooked or bolted. Certainly, the fastenings are out of reach of a child, usually on the flat top of the cornice, and the hook is of iron, but the change of intention is significant.

From 1800 until about 1830, therefore, we find the strong, plain house, very solidly made, thinly painted to represent stone or stucco. It is usually about 4ft (1.2m) high and 3ft (90cm) wide with three, sometimes four, rooms and no staircase; the front opens in one wing and the sides are fitted with heavy iron handles. The windows have single panes, sometimes painted to represent four. The stout dresser in the kitchen is hardly ever pulled away; if it has been, the interior looks very dull, for originally even chimney-pieces were sometimes left out, but as a plaything it must have been perfect. It is almost indestructible, it could not tip over and a child – the tiny child whose muslin dress and satin shoe charm and trouble us now – could easily have crept inside it. Sometimes one side of the roof is made to lift up, or there is a drawer in a low plinth, and this gives space for space furniture or for a change of curtains, a most useful and desirable arrangement.

By now, it is clear that dolls' houses have been made commercially for some years by artisan 'chamber masters', selling their wares to toyshops, or with the materials supplied by the retailer, who would take the finished toy. The eighteenth-century toyman who advertised baby houses and their furniture cannot have kept many of the largest in stock at one time. Contemporary illustrations show very small houses, and in the last few years some of these have been identified, including one marked by the toyman Bellamy, who had premises in Holborn from the 1760s, which has furniture, not to

scale, from the same shop. At a later period, a tiny house is also shown in the well-known engraving of the Lowther Arcade in the 1850s.

Dolls' houses of the 1850s and 1860s are notable for very elaborate and well-made façades, the pillars, mouldings, rustication and so forth beautifully executed, but the interior is badly proportioned, skimped in detail, often with absurdly low doors (unpanelled), mean chimney-pieces and a squalid steep staircase or none. There is sometimes a stand, roughly made in contrast to the cabinetwork on the façade, but this is not usual. Houses of the 1870s are much smaller and the stand returns; they are given supports precisely like the wash-hand stands of the period – they are not in fact wash-hand stands, as I believed when I first saw an example, but carefully made and braced so that the house drops into it. An oddity peculiar to this time is that houses are sometimes backless (see pages 139–43, Shell Villa); the front is either a fixed one or lifts off in one piece and a curtain or a spring-blind keeps out the dust at the back. At first sight, this seems a practical arrangement, but it makes the placing of the furniture very difficult. The reader agrees, surely, that there is something disconcerting when through the windows above the front door one sees a red rep curtain instead of flowered wallpaper?

It is difficult to take an interest in the English commercial dolls' house made at the latter end of the nineteenth century, usually in the form known as 'box-back'. The walls are thin and the paper has slit over the cracks in the deal; there is a perfunctory indication of stone or brick and all the workmanship is expended on bay windows of unpleasant proportions; the kitchen is always the nicest room in the house.

THE OPENING

The best guide in dating a baby house is the thickness of the walls and the look of solidity. Since this is a matter of proportion, it can be appreciated better after looking at a number of houses, especially from the sides and the back, where the eye is not distracted by the detail of the façade. Look for evidence of painstaking carpentry: carefully made roof-ridges, for instance, and separately carved tiles. Handmade iron handles at the sides can confirm tentative dating and occasionally fine iron strapwork hinges or brass butterfly hinges survive. These, however, take the brunt of the wear and have very often been replaced by others later than the house itself. Internal doors sometimes have their leather hinges intact or they swing on small brass ones held by a pin, and old screws can be easily distinguished if it is possible to withdraw them, for they had no points.

The fastenings of the baby houses are extremely interesting. It is hardly credible how a box with four sides can be planned with so many different methods of opening. The Georgian House (see pages 24–6) referred to earlier, for instance, has wings at each end, both of which locked. The front does not open at all and the ingenious staircase goes up between double walls, disappearing from view and only partly visible when the library door on the first floor is opened. At Nostell Priory the front slides apart, another house rises on sash cord like a window, and many mid-Victorian houses, as I have said, have a façade that simply lifts off, or else an immovable front is combined with an open back. Then again, others open on all four sides, as at Longleat. A dolls' house in Sherborne Museum has an astonishing arrangement by which smaller rooms lead out of the front rooms, and are seen through a doorway. At first one cannot imagine how the furniture arrived there; in fact, it is accessible by an inconspicuous door on the outside wall. A similar complex structure can be seen in the Cedars, Woodbridge (see pages 168–71).

STAIRCASES

In domestic architecture until 1700 stairs were built in short straight flights of six or eight steps, then a quarter-landing and another flight, but by the early eighteenth century the flights increased in length to twelve or sixteen or even more steps and the treads and risers were sometimes inlaid in patterns, showing that no stair carpet was used as yet, and there were often winders. Finally, in the late eighteenth century we have the lovely elliptical 'flying' staircase, turning from floor to floor with no landings and all winders, the handrails being in one continuous length from top to bottom. In the Regency these stairs were often of stone, with delicate ironwork banisters topped by a round mahogany rail. Banisters had been growing more and more slender, often grouped in threes on a step, the bases ending on the edge of steps instead of on strings as formerly. Since early baby houses may be expected to possess only an indicated or a half-staircase, and late houses, after 1800, to be without any, it follows that the best examples occur, on the whole, between 1740 and 1790. In this book Cane End House (see pages 42–7) is the finest we have. A small house may have a characteristic staircase, whereas a comparatively elaborate nineteenth-century example, such as the Bidder House

(see pages 125–31), will have a perfunctory attempt or none. With very few exceptions the beautiful stairways, some of them fine enough for textbook models, belong to the mid-eighteenth century.

WINDOWS

The proportions of rooms are often strangely altered. Victorian dolls' houses always have rooms too high for their size; eighteenth-century ones often have ceilings lower than might be expected. The late dolls' houses, mass-manufactured, are the worst proportioned, and many of us have puzzled over the arrangement of furniture in a room 12 by 10in (30 x 25cm), but 15in (38cm) high. In life, the only room shaped like this would be a bathroom; in an eighteenth-century house it would probably be a passage room lined with shelves for the display of china.

Windows are to be found cut in fanciful shapes, lunettes or exact squares, and without reference to suitability or sometimes to the interior lighting; but usually they are in the manner to be expected from their façade – nine-paned, twelve-paned or a triple Venetian window, or sometimes bricked up or painted black. In the Regency period there are rare occurrences of the pointed Gothick Revival windows, as at Regency Gothick (see pages 72–9), and Strawberry Hill Gothick (see pages 89–91), and then the unique chinoiserie windows of Coburg (see pages 119–24).

DOORS AND CHIMNEY-PIECES

Reference has been made to the beauty of detail in the mid-eighteenth-century examples. The test of an 'interesting' baby house of any period is the workmanship of doors and surrounds. The best doors are panelled and fitted with brass handles, round or drop-shaped, and occasionally even with finger-plates, keyholes and escutcheons. Front doors are panelled with moulded frames and returns. They have a real lock and a centre knob or a knocker in brass. In the nineteenth-century examples the knocker is sometimes a lion's head with a ring in its mouth; earlier ones bear a wreath or plain ring. A charming addition found once or twice is a plate with the owner's name engraved on it. From 1870 onward the commercially made dolls' houses have badly proportioned doors, too small and too square. They are frequently covered or padded in felt or baize, or in stamped leather or a kind of embossed brown paper like Lincrusta, unattractive and grimy.

FIREPLACES, GRATES AND WOODWORK

These are dealt with more fully when the individual houses are described. An early eighteenth-century house will have a square opening, painted black, where a free-standing basket grate once stood; when these survive they are usually in cast brass (see Strawberry Hill Gothick, pages 89–91). In a real house there would be a carved chimney-piece above it, probably enclosing a picture, and in Van Haeften House (see pages 33–5), a baby-house example survives. Where it is lacking, a small landscape in a wide frame gives a good effect.

Many houses of the later eighteenth century still have their delightful hob grates, perhaps flanked by reeded pilasters or half-round columns. A house of George II's reign that I have seen has one fireplace with free-standing pillars marbled to match the chimney-piece above it, but all the others have been pulled out and Victorian grates substituted. These stamped tin-plate or cast-iron grates are in themselves extremely attractive and were made from about 1800 until late in the century in the same Regency patterns. It is now known that many of the tinplate models were made by Evans and Cartwright of Wolverhampton. The cast-iron examples were sometimes made as chimney ornaments for real houses and adapted for dolls' houses. German 'lead' grates and chimney-pieces all in one were made in a fragile kind of trelliswork by the firm of Babette Schweizer of Diessen and were imported from the 1850s. They have an attraction, too, being often brushed with colour – poison-bottle blue, red or gold – but are for some reason always too small in scale for English dolls' houses.

A moulded cornice is a sign of good workmanship; skirtings are another sign of careful joinery and all doors should have frames and be panelled. Wainscoting on the walls is, of course, frequently seen in eighteenth-century baby houses (though stamped papier mâché sometimes imitates it in the Regency and Lincrusta in the 1880s). The substitute appears to have been used in real houses also, and at an early date, for in 1805 Joseph Farington admired the royal apartments at Windsor: 'The hangings scarlet, and the paper stained to have the effect of wainscot, very well done.' Lady Luxborough, in a letter to Shenstone, refers to Prince Hoare, the sculptor who took on general decoration at Bath, *circa* 1750, and says: 'although a Statuary he deigns to exercise his art in sculpture on humble paper ceilings, which are very handsome.' This, too, sounds like papier mâché.

GLOSSARY

The descriptive text of this book uses some terms in describing architectural features, types of doll, dolls' house and dolls'-house furniture which it would be awkward to explain in context, especially when they occur frequently. Some further information, in case it is needed, is included here.

baby house 'Baby' was the word used up to the early nineteenth century for a doll of any kind, hence 'baby house'. The term is used here to describe the large, architectural houses of the eighteenth and early nineteenth centuries, commissioned as individual items from joiners or carpenters and very often intended for adult amusement. Because the contents might be valuable – for example, including silver – they had usually a lock or locks to protect the contents. They are thus distinguished from the toy houses made commercially for children, of the same or later periods.

baluster A small pillar, usually in a row supporting a coping or handrail. On an interior staircase, called a banister.

Biedermeier An artistic and decorative style, popular in Germany, Austria, etc. from *circa* 1815–48. It was characterized in furniture by simplicity, comfort, curving lines, little use of surface decoration and the use of mahogany, rosewood, birch, etc. veneers. Early Waltershausen dolls'-house furniture reflected this style, and, because of the conservatism of the manufacturers, later pieces continued to be made in the same style, although in declining quality, until the end of the century.

bisque A fine porcelain with a matt surface used for dolls' heads, etc. during the nineteenth century, especially in France and Germany. Many dolls'-house dolls were made in Germany by firms such as Hertwig from this material. Dolls with glazed porcelain heads are usually described as 'china'.

box-back Type of commercially made dolls' house, made in England from the late eighteenth century to 1930, in which a usually flat façade projects above a rectangular box. They vary greatly in size and quality, and were based on a common type of London town house of the eighteenth century onwards. First identified in the catalogue of a late Victorian wholesaler, Messrs Silber and Fleming, but made by a variety of small East End cabinetmakers, the so-called 'chamber masters', over this very long period.

Bubb, John An early nineteenth-century maker of dolls' and dolls'-house furniture, including chests of drawers, cabinets, tilt-top and drop-leaf tables, bureaux, etc. made of or stained as mahogany. His work is clearly marked with an impressed stamp '*john bubb maker*'. In business *circa* 1810–40, in Long Lane, Bermondsey, London.

chair rail Also called a dado rail, a moulding fixed to a wall at the height of a chairback, to protect the wall from damage, especially at the period when chairs were usually ranged along the wall when not actually in use.

cornice A term in classical architecture, used to mean a moulded edge along the top of a building or, indoors, at the junction of wall and ceiling.

dado The area of wall above the skirting board in a room, usually marked at its upper edge by a moulding, called a chair rail or dado rail.

dentil moulding A series of small blocks, projecting beneath a classical cornice.

dog-leg staircase A staircase in which the flights run parallel to each other, without a stairwell.

doors A door is set into a wooden doorcase or frame. Six panels are usual in an eighteenth-century door, and these can been fielded (raised) or sunk. Four panels are usual in the later nineteenth century. Doors were almost invariably painted, or grained to imitate more expensive woods.

drizzle Drizzling was an occupation of ladies, and sometimes gentlemen (including Queen Victoria's Uncle Leopold), involving cutting to pieces gold braid and embroidery to obtain and sell the gold metal. It was one of the most destructive and boring hobbies ever conceived.

Dutch oven A tinplate cooking utensil which is used in front of an open fire, to cook small items.

Erzgebirge A mountainous area in Saxony, Germany, famous since the eighteenth century for its manufacture of wooden toys of all sorts, turned and carved. Here were made dolls' houses, dolls'-house furniture (oftenly of a slightly less sophisticated kind than in Thüringia), sets of turned dishes in oval boxes, etc. The manufacture of wooden toys continues in village such as Seiffen to the present time.

Evans and Cartwright A toy firm, the only large nineteenth-century English tinplate toy manufacturerer, in operation from *circa* 1800–1880, making metal dolls'-house furniture in Regency and William IV styles, in Wolverhampton in the West Midlands. Now known to be the maker of the tinplate furniture mentioned in Vivien Greene's earlier books as having once been called 'Auley'. Their output included living-room, bedroom, nursery, hall and kitchen pieces, as well as fireplaces and probably most of the specifically English kitchen equipment, such as meat-screens. Their furniture items were hand-painted and stoved, using the same process as used for japanned (*tole*) ware such as trays. The firm was founded by John Evans, who later took into partnership his stepson Sidney Cartwright. Cartwright was responsible for the development and success of the factory from the 1820s onwards.

façade The front face of a building.

fillet An edging, often metal used as a border for wall coverings. A term in classical architecture for a narrow element of a cornice.

Grödnertal A valley in a mountainous part of northern Italy, which became the centre of production of carved, jointed wooden dolls, exported in quantity from the early nineteenth century. The early dolls have great charm, with hand-painted heads, often with yellow combs in their hair, and made in sizes suitable for dolls' houses. Those dressed by Princess Victoria and her governess Baroness Lehzen are preserved in the London Museum.

jib door A door flush with the wall and often disguised by being papered over or covered with false books in a library.

half-tester A type of bed in which a canopy extends over the head of the bed only.

hastener See **meat-screen**

hood mould Also called a dripstone: a moulding over a window to deflect rainwater, used in early English houses, and also in the nineteenth-century 'Tudor' revival houses.

jack A device for turning meat while it roasts on an open fire. Type 1: a pendulum weight on a chain descends slowly, causing a clockwork mechanism on the wall to turn a spit. Type 2: a smoke jack, used in larger kitchens, where heated air from the fire turns a fan in the chimney to power the turning spit. Type 3: a bottle jack, a brass cylinder containing clockwork, with a hook from which the meat hangs while turning, often used inside a meat-screen. Other devices to turn spits, including little boys and small dogs, were superseded by these jacks. Wax jacks were small devices for holding a length of wax, used on writing desks for sealing letters.

Lauscha A small hill town in Thuringia, Germany, famous for its glass industry from the seventeenth century to the present day. A craft industry, it produced a wide variety of items such as glass eyes for dolls and humans, Christmas decorations, etc. Much of the nineteenth-century dolls'-house ware, made in milky glass and hand-decorated with flowers etc., came from here.

Palladian A style of classical architecture named after the Renaissance Italian architect Palladio. First introduced in Britain in the seventeenth century by Inigo Jones, it was popularized in the early eighteenth century by Lord Burlington. Its characteristics are the adoption of the proportions and features of classical Rome, especially of temples, and porticoes and pediments appear on houses as well as churches. It quickly became, in the hands of Burlington, Campbell, John Wood, etc. the dominating style and was widely employed for country houses in England until late in the century.

pediment In classical architecture a triangular feature above a portico, or above a window or doorway.

pewter An alloy of lead and tin. However, it is used in this book as a convenient term to describe a variety of alloys of unknown composition containing lead used by toymakers to make dolls'-house metalware and furniture, usually stamped or cast.

pilaster A classical column attached to a wall, rectangular in section, usually conforming to one of the five orders of classical architecture.

posy A short motto, usually engraved on the inside of a ring.

quoins, quoining Rectangular stone dressings usually along the corner edges of buildings and usually alternately long and short.

rustication A treatment of masonry walls in which the stones are emphasized by heavily sunken joints and/or roughened surfaces. A feature of Palladian architecture.

sanitary wallpaper A type of Victorian wallpaper machine-printed in oil colours, often with a varnished surface, which was 'washable' and hence advertised as healthy, common from the 1870s onwards.

straw-work A form of mosaic decoration using coloured straws, used to decorate fancy goods, including toys. Noah's Arks are often found covered in it. It was widely used, in England most notably by the French prisoners in the Napoleonic wars, their work being particularly well represented in Peterborough Museum.

string The structural parts of a staircase which carry the ends of the steps (treads and risers).

string course A moulded band running across a wall horizontally, often marking the top of one storey.

Tunbridge The town of Tunbridge Wells in Kent was a resort from the seventeenth century onwards and developed an industry making souvenir ware in turned woods. Late eighteenth-century pieces are often hand-painted in naïve red, green, etc. designs. In the nineteenth century the town became famous for wood mosaic, and the pieces included miniature tables, etc. often found in dolls' houses.

Venetian window A feature of Palladian architecture, three windows grouped together, the centre window round-topped and larger than the other two, much used in eighteenth-century houses.

Waltershausen A manufacturing town in Thüringia, known for the dolls made by the firm of Kestner and others. It was also the centre of production of dolls'-house furniture of the highest quality, including the well-known imitation-rosewood style, often decorated with gilt transfers. The range of products was immense, with some hundreds of designs, each produced in two or three wood finishes and up to nine graduated scales. Manufacture seems to have begun in the 1840s, with the Biedermeier-style pieces, and to have continued, with the addition of later styles in different finishes, until at least the First World War. Vivien Greene's visit to Waltershausen to establish the origin of this furniture is described on pages 13–15.

winder The tapered tread where a staircase turns a corner.

woolwork Used in this book to describe needlework in wool completely covering a canvas base; Berlin woolwork was a version popular in the early nineteenth century, for which hand-coloured printed patterns were supplied by German suppliers. Now often called needlepoint tapestry.

SELECT BIBLIOGRAPHY

This booklist is limited to a few books which deal authoritatively with dolls' houses and furniture of the eighteenth and nineteenth centuries; the earlier books are mainly out of print but are obtainable through libraries.

Ackerman, Evelyn, *The Genius of Moritz Gottschalk*, Gold Horse Publishing, Annapolis, Maryland, USA, 1994
New survey of principal German manufactuer of commercial houses

Eaton, Faith, *The Ultimate Dolls' House Book*, Dorling Kindersley, London, 1994
Illustrated book dealing with all countries and periods

Greene, Vivien, *English Dolls' Houses of the Eighteenth and Nineteenth Centuries*, B. T. Batsford Ltd, London, 1955 (another edition Bell and Hyman, 1979)

Family Dolls' House, G. Bell and Sons, London, 1973

Himmelheber, Georg, *Kleine Möbel*, Deutsche Kunst Verlag, München, 1979
Early miniature furniture mainly doll-size
(German text)

Jacobs, Flora Gill, *A History of Dolls' Houses*, Cassell, 1954 (another revised edition Charles Scribner's Sons, New York, 1965)

Dolls' Houses in America Charles Scribner's Sons, New York, 1974
The definitive book on American houses, including some British immigrants

Victorian Dolls' Houses and Their Furnishings, Washington Dolls' House and Toy Museum, 1978

King, Constance Eileen, *The Collector's History of Dolls' Houses*, Robert Hale Ltd, London, 1983
Comprehensive book, some attributions superseded by later research

Towner, Margaret, *Dolls' House Furniture*, The Apple Press, London, and Courage Books, Philadelphia, 1983
Furniture from the seventeenth to twentieth centuries

Wilckens, Leonie von, *Mansions in Miniature*, Viking Press, New York, 1980
Translation of *Das Puppenhaus*, dealing especially with early German houses